## Your Guide to
# MODELLING FRENCH RAILWAYS
## CM FRENCH SPECIAL

We hope you will enjoy and be inspired by this French Special, our fifth geographically-themed extra edition. The railways of France are frequently the subject of articles in CONTINENTAL MODELLER, but this Special allows us to present longer features, in more detail, and with more and larger pictures than would usually be possible in a regular issue of the magazine.

When considering what to include in this guide, we decided that the best way to illustrate the current state of modelling French railways was with the work of modellers, in Britain and on the continent. CM has a long tradition of using contributors from Europe, and the majority of the articles here are from French modellers. We are fortunate that we have quite a stock of quality material; selecting what to include was quite a task, and (as with the German and Swiss specials of previous years – both still available) we could easily have produced twice as much, had time and economics allowed.

In a relatively modest volume such as this, we can only hope to provide an introduction, to give a flavour, and to show something of the appeal of modelling French railways. It is quite a large country, encompassing many different landscapes, with a wide range of railway operations past and present.

We have tried to feature a mixture of scales and gauges, and layouts large and small, to cater for all tastes, and resources.

These features are supported by some prototype background and layout suggestions, and augmented with practical modelling tips.

Those interested in the railways of France are fortunate to have the support of an excellent special interest group: the French Railways Society (until recently the SNCF Society).

Due to the general lack of foreign language skills in Britain, such societies have an important role in translating sources of information.

The Society publishes a fine quarterly journal, by no means restricted to modelling, which also provides (through reports from members) travel advice for those who wish to go and experience French railways for themselves.

The railways in France have a long history: the first line opened as early as 1828. Wanting to direct transport policy, the government passed a law in 1842 determining the basis of the future network. The state would supply the land and all civil engineering which it would then lease to companies that would lay the track and run the trains. By the 1850s, major routes had coalesced into the 'Big Six' grands réseaux – Est, Nord, Ouest, Paris–Orléans, Midi (in the south), and Paris–Lyon–Méditerranée. Later, lines of general and local interest were promoted, for which metre gauge was widely used, as much for economy as its ability to traverse difficult country. It is claimed that at one time you could travel the length of the country – albeit slowly! – on secondary lines, but most succumbed to competition from motor vehicles. In 1938 the railways were nationalised as the Société Nationale des Chemins de Fer français (SNCF).

The national railway museum, the Cité du Train, at Mulhouse, is excellent. There is some preservation in the form of museum lines, but operation by volunteers can be erratic; timetables often seem to be arranged around a long pause for lunch – very civilised! There are also commercially run tourist lines, often using heritage stock, on former SNCF lines in scenically attractive areas.

As elsewhere, the dominant scale/gauge is HO, and the focus of attention is Epoch III to the present day. The main domestic manufacturer is Jouef, now part of the Hornby International group, and several specialists have emerged in recent years offering high quality ready-to-run models (produced in China) – brands such as LS Models, REE Modèles, R37, Modelbex, and Mistral.

Swiss-based specialists as Fulgurex and Lemaco (now Lematec) have also seen the potential of the French market for their high quality limited edition metal models, and we should now add Eisenbahn Canada to that category.

Major European manufacturers such as Roco, Piko, and Märklin/Trix have long recognised the potential of the French market, and as a result French stock is quite well represented not only in HO but also in N; TT and Z are not common. As elsewhere, O has been on the rise in recent years, though it remains the preserve of specialists. Reflecting the prototype situation, metre gauge subjects have had some commercial support, mostly as kits in HOm, with some Om and a little Nm. Industrial narrow gauge also has a certain following.

French mainstream models are quite easily available from several specialist outlets in Britain, most of whom advertise regularly in CONTINENTAL MODELLER. However, in common with many markets now, production runs – even from the large manufacturers – may be limited, so it is well worth ordering when new items are announced and accepting that there may be quite a wait for delivery.

So, here is a selective look at French railway modelling – we trust that you find it interesting and entertaining.

## A brief guide to the 'Epoch/Era' dating system

As a convenient way of defining broad periods of railway history across Europe, the following terms are generally used:

EPOCH I – approximately 1870 to 1920;
    vehicles in the liveries of the separate state and private railways.
EPOCH II – approximately 1920 to 1945,
    from the formation of the large national state networks
    (DRG, BBÖ, SBB, etc).
EPOCH III – approximately 1945 to 1968.
EPOCH IV – approximately 1968 to 1994;
    vehicles with UIC computer numbering.
EPOCH V – 1994 to 2006, from the foundation of DBAG,
    the formation of private railway operating companies
    and Europe-wide liberalisation of railway traffic.
EPOCH VI – introduction of new Europe-wide UIC vehicle numbers
    containing a country-specific code, starting 2007.

## Scale and gauge comparison

| | UK | gauge (model) | Europe | | gauge represented |
|---|---|---|---|---|---|
| Z | 1:220 | 6.5mm | 1:220 | Z | standard |
| no equivalent | | 6.5mm | 1:160 | Nm | metre |
| N | 1:148 | 9mm | 1:160 | N | standard |
| TT | 1:100 | 12mm | 1:120 | TT | standard |
| OO | 1:76 | 16.5mm | 1:87 | HO | standard |
| no equivalent | | 6.5mm | 1:87 | HOf | 60cm |
| OO9 | 1:76 | 9mm | 1:87 | HOe | 75/76cm |
| OOn3 | 1:76 | 12mm | 1:87 | HOm | metre |
| O | 1:43.5 | 32mm | 1:45 | O | standard |
| O-16.5 | 1:43.5 | 16.5mm | 1:45 | Oe | 75/76cm |
| no equivalent | | 22.2mm | 1:45 | Om | metre |
| 1 | 1:32 | 45mm | 1:32 | 1 | standard |
| G | 1:22.5 | 45mm | 1:22.5 | G | metre |

*Your Guide to*
# MODELLING FRENCH RAILWAYS

## CM FRENCH SPECIAL

# Contents

48

86

| | |
|---|---|
| **Editor** | Andrew Burnham |
| **Assistant Editor** | Tim Rayner |
| **Associate Editor & Photographer** | Steve Flint |
| **Editorial Assistant & Photographer** | Craig Tiley |
| **Art Director** | Adrian Stickland |
| **Graphic Illustration** | Dave Clements, Gary Bickley, Steve Croucher |
| **General & Advertisement Manager** | John King |
| **Direct Subscriptions** | Alicia Flint |
| **Editorial Director** | Ben Arnold |

ISBN 978 0 900586 62 0    *ref*.PM-211    © Peco Publications & Publicity Ltd. 2019

Printed by: William Gibbons & Sons Ltd., P.O.Box 103, 26, Planetary Road, Willenhall, West Midlands, WV13 3XT.

Distribution to the newsagency trade (Home & Overseas): Marketforce (UK), Second Floor, 5, Churchill Place, Canary Wharf, London, E14 5HU.

On a scenic route which carries heavy traffic

# Orelle-Prémont

**Thomas Gallé** has modelled a distinctive mountain line in HO.

Above
**The TER (regional express) to Modane
formed by a Z2 electric multiple unit
emerges from the tunnel to Chambéry and Lyon.**

# The genesis

Coming originally from Orléans in the centre of France, it was not until 2005 that I discovered the so-called "Maurienne" line between Chambéry and the border station at Modane. This line links Lyon and Savoy in France to Milan and Piedmont in Italy with freight and passenger traffic. The Maurienne line was one of the most important in France for freight traffic from the 1970s to the 1990s. It was originally electrified with third rail and converted to overhead catenary in 1976. The route has steep gradients of more than 3% requiring double heading and banking to allow heavier trains to cross the Alps.

In the mid-2000s, this route had the advantage of seeing a wide variety of regional, main line, and FRET equipment. For a few years the old locos from the 1960s and 1970s still rubbed shoulders with modern machines and TGVs.

I became particularly interested in the remarkable site of Orelle-Prémont. At this point the line winds through a narrow valley, making its way between the old national road and the river while the unsightly new motorway is hidden in a tunnel. I immediately had the idea of representing this section in a layout one day. However, construction did not begin until ten years later.

Below
**A Corail train in the valley.**

Above
**The Alpine Motorway (AFA) piggy-back service climbs the Maurienne towards Italy hauled by a pair of BB36000 Bo-Bo electrics either side of the lorry drivers' coach.**

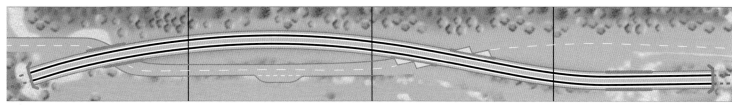

## Planning

The plan is based on satellite photos and on-site surveys. Some compression and modifications were necessary to fit the site into the space that I had available. For example, it has been necessary to increase the radii of the curves whereas the great majority of the modellers are tempted to do the opposite. This is necessary to limit the depth of the modules and thus facilitate handling, transport, and storage. Along with ease of assembly these are the main concerns during the design of a layout that you wish to exhibit.

To enhance the scenery, the layout was built in 'showcases' which most importantly allow ideal lighting of the scene and optimal protection of the scenery during transport.

The track is 1.30m above the ground. This offers good visibility for adults and allows younger viewers to watch the passage of trains from below, with a perspective close to the real thing, thanks to the stepped topography of the site.

## The structure

This project is a team effort, done with my father. Construction began in January 2016. My father, a professional industrial designer and amateur carpenter, directed the design and manufacture of the base, the showcases, and the storage sidings at the back, then I took on the technical part (track and wiring) and shaping the landscape.

We started with the construction of the four modules which make up the base. Each one is independent to facilitate assembly. Each leg supports two modules, which means there is less scope for mis-alignment. We then installed the trackbed in the four modules, ensuring perfect alignment.

Above
An intermodal train for Modane
hauled by a Euro Cargo Rail
TRAXX Bo-Bo electric.

Inset
The train of Corail coaches
is headed by a BB26000 Bo-Bo electric.

## The track

The track is Peco *bi-bloc* concrete code 75, laid with 1mm superelevation on the curves. This was achieved by sliding plasticard tabs under the outer rail. The transitions were obtained by gradually reducing the thickness of these tabs.

The track was weathered with an airbrush after ballasting. Detailing of the track features a wide range of products from French specialist craftsmen, using whitemetal casting, photo-etching, and 3D-printing.

## The scenery

The landscape was made conventionally of expanded polystyrene cut with a heated wire and reworked with a cutter.

The majority of the retaining walls are based on Faller N gauge products, repainted, coated, and weathered. The rest of the walls and structures, such as bridges and tunnels, were made from wooden sections, cardboard, plasticard, and foamboard.

The rocks are a combination of assembled plaster casts and carvings in plaster applied in bulk. They were weathered with washes of acrylic paints.

The omnipresent road in the valley was simulated by a thin layer of plaster worked to represent the texture and defects of the worn tarmac surface.

The vegetation is mainly from the Heki range (fibres, grass mats, and foliage nets). Around 1,200 trees were made from sea foam and covered with a particular type of foliage from Busch. To obtain four shades of colour, this medium green material was tinted with a few drops of acrylic paint mixed with the flock in an electric coffee grinder.

The river bed was made from sand and crushed and tinted limestone. After several tries, I focussed on a combination of two ways to represent the water. I applied five thin coats of resin coloured with a few drops of acrylic paint, each layer being between 2 and 3mm thick. A textured Woodland Scenics gel was then used to represent waves and eddies.

Above left
**Two trackside photographers salute the train driver.**

Above
**A characteristic angled bridge crossing the old national route 6.**

Right
**A Z82500 four-car bi-mode *Autorail à Grande Capacité* (AGC) crosses the River Arc.**

Below
**A freight train bound for Lyon descends the valley behind a classic BB7200.**

Below
**A catenary mast with a double arm.**

Below
**Two catenary masts with different types of single arm.**

Below
**A catenary mast with a double arm.**

Below
**Two catenary masts with different types of single arm.**

## The catenary

The catenary was soldered up on jigs from 0.3mm and 0.4mm diameter nickel-silver wire, each span being made to measure depending on the location of the posts. These were made from brass section and photo-etched parts. The whole was then painted and weathered.

The catenary is slightly stretched so that it is straight and taut, but nevertheless the pantographs on the locos are fixed 2mm below the contact wire to protect it from any pulling.

The catenary remains in place during transport and storage; only the sections over the board joins are removed.

## The hidden sidings and operation

The four scenic modules are supplied by ten tracks behind the scenes, five for each direction.

The wiring allows each circuit to be controlled independently, regardless of supply – analogue, conventional digital, or digital with block signalling, controlled by a computer. In that mode it is possible to run up to twelve trains randomly and automatically.

## Conclusion

The layout was completed in September 2018, so took a little less than three years of work by two people. It was specifically designed to be shown at exhibitions, where we aim to operate authentic trains for different periods (advised in signs at each end of the layout) in a convincing environment.

Left
Maintenance work on the signal.

Photographs by the editor.

Above
The intermodal train for Modane crossing the old RN 6.

Top
The TGV for Paris on the bridge.

Inset
Maintenance work on a signal.

A large station with operating potential

# Neussargues

**Ian Stock** explores an interesting location.
*Photographs as credited. Drawings by the author.*

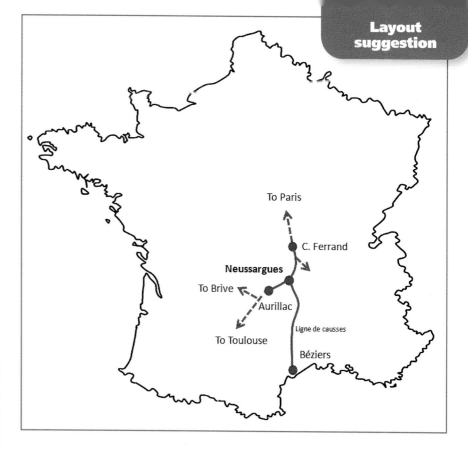

Below
**Neussargues today: X2819 + XR6091 + X2914 en route from Langogne (08.15) to Le Lioran (11.51) on 28th July 2018.**
Photo: Gwenaël Piérart.

Below right
**An old postcard of Neussargues in its heyday, served by trains from both the Orléans and Midi companies.**

Neussarges in the depths of the Cantal in the Massif Central is a through station that functions in part as a terminus, where a series of straggling single-track cross-country lines meet, relatively in the middle of nowhere to form quite a large railway node.

The oddness of Neussargues-Moissac was apparent from the moment we approached: I already knew that there was a sizeable railway station in the vicinity, but we almost missed the turning off the main road, down a narrow lane to a settlement whose current population is just over 900, and which peaked in the 1960s at 1,250 – many of whom must have been railway employees. Hardly a metropolis.

Set in the shallow valley of the Alagnon river and surrounded by tree-clad ridges, it is a scattered sort of a place, with not much by way of a discernible centre. But it is mostly well-kept, and it is easy to forget that one is at an altitude of 810 metres (2,600 feet) above sea level, where there is significant snowfall in winter. There remains a small row of shops along the road next to the station, a large church, and several other imposing buildings scattered over quite a wide area. It is pleasant enough, in a rather back-woods kind of a way – and it has a claim to fame, as the composer Olivier Messiaen composed some of his finest works while staying in a friend's chateau here.

NEUSSARGUES GARE (Alt. 806 m.)
Vue d'ensemble de la Gare des C⁺ d'Orléans et du Midi

LE CANTAL ILLUSTR
4455

LE CANTAL PITTORESQUE     425. NEUSSARGUES — La Gare

Left and below left
**Two old cards which illustrate the development of the station: the upper view shows the original Paris-Orléans 1866 building and track arrangement, the lower picture the larger structure erected after the Midi arrived in 1888.**

And then there is the station itself: far out of all proportion to the settlement it serves, it had six platform faces, four of which retain their track, if not their trains, and alongside, a marshalling yard of perhaps a dozen tracks. A little out of sight at the east end of the station is the remains of a large motive power depot, which retains a working turntable, for steam specials operate here from time to time. And perhaps most bizarre of all in such a place, the station is fully wired with a spider's web of vintage 1,500V DC catenary, for this is the northern limit of the celebrated electrified *Ligne de Causses* which winds its way up from the coast at Béziers, by way of Millau and St.Flour.

The other main line serving the station is the west–east route from Aurillac to Clermont Ferrand, which sees trains originating at both Brive la Gaillarde and Toulouse and heading north-eastwards along the long straggling single-track route over the high pass and ski resort at Le Lioran, which lies some way to the west.

At the time of writing, it was hard to determine whether the *Ligne de Causses* was really still open or not; there appeared to be one train per day each way between Clermont Ferrand and Béziers, but all other services had been replaced by buses. Closure had been announced in 2016, amid some outcry, and by early 2019 there were suggestions that new military activity in the area was going to need to be rail-served. It is a sad prospect to consider the huge Eiffel-built Viaduc de Garabit south of St.Flour, which is a national monument, completely devoid of trains.

L'Auvergne Pittoresque     1848. NEUSSARGUES — La Gare

Left
**The station building as it is now -– not much has changed.**
Photo: Papou Poustache.

Below left and below
**Looking east along the platform towards the Clermont and Béziers lines.**
Photos: Ian Stock.

Above right:
**Peak services: three X73500 units connecting at the station.**
Photo: Papou Poustache.

Right:
**Preserved X3800 'Picasso' Nº4039 working from Aurillac (13.50) to Saint-Flour–Chaudes-Aigues (17.35) on 28th July 2018.**
Photo: Gwenaël Piérart.

The *Ligne de Causses* was electrified as long ago as 1932, no doubt on account of its punishing gradients. (Causses are limestone plateaux, which give the northern end of the route a rather bleak, windswept appearance.) Further south, near Millau, it passes under Norman Foster's distinctive new motorway viaduct, the highest in the world. But alas, the line appears to be suffering a slow death.

As a result of all this activity, Neussargues was provided with a huge station, which has become increasingly far too much for local needs. It still has a regular, roughly hourly service between Aurillac and Clermont, but most of the famed activity is gone. The key to this was the fact that the lines from Clermont and Béziers arrive in the station from

But back to Neussargues itself. The west–east route from Aurillac was the first to arrive, and the station opened in 1866, served by the expansionist Paris-Orléans Railway. The station became a junction in 1888, with the arrival of the Compagnie du Midi route from St.Flour and Béziers, and its importance grew. Marshalling yards were installed to facilitate the exchange of traffic between the two lines. The Béziers route became a secondary through route from Paris to the south coast, via Clermont – and indeed its one remaining train retains the name *L'Aubrac*, which was the flagship train on the line – although it has now been cut back far short of Paris.

In late 1907, the station gained another route, with the arrival of the steeply-graded, rather vertiginous, branch line from Bort-les-Orgues to the north, joining the Aurillac route just to the west of the station. This line eventually closed in 1990, but was known for a long time for its specialist live-stock trains. A section of it is now operated as a preserved line, complete with classic X2800 *autorail*.

Left
**X2819 + XR6091 + X2914
leaving Neussargues for
Le Lioran, 28th July 2018.**
Photo: Gwenaël Piérart.

Below left
**A BB67300 arriving from
Aurillac with a short train
of four Corail coaches.**
Photo: P.Poustache collection.

Below
**X 72653 forming a regional
express leaves Neussargues.**
Photo: Papou Poustache.

Below right
**Harking back to the days of
electric loco-hauled trains:
BB4230 waits as parcels
are loaded into the van.**

Below left and below
**The buildings along the road
parallel to the line would
make an attractive backdrop.**

the same easterly direction, the former climbing sharply up
the valley of the Alagnon, while the latter sweeps equally
steeply down out of the hills, the gradients only easing at the
station throat. Thus any through traffic between Clermont
and Béziers needed to reverse – and in the days when electric trains were still running, also change traction. Since the
north- and south-bound *Aubrac* services (latterly formed of
just three or four Corail coaches) also crossed in the station,
once a day it awoke from its semi-slumber to become a hive
of activity for around twenty minutes, while locomotives
were changed and passengers swapped between trains on
the two main routes. In both cases, the diesel locomotives
also ran light to and from Aurillac for the manoeuvre.

A good video of the procedure, filmed in 2006 when the
train was still running to and from Paris, can be seen at:

https://www.youtube.com/watch?v=Hb8EAcxEnuo

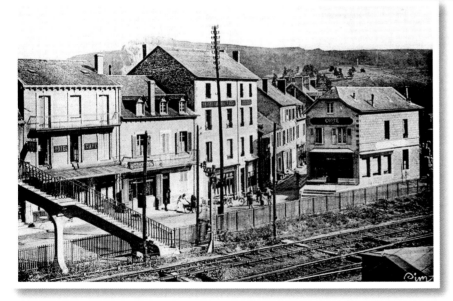

Nowadays, virtually all trains are X73500 *autorails*, with
occasional X72500 or X76000 two- or three- car replacements, as can be seen in this more recent video:

www.youtube.com/watch?time_continue=529&v=jEBklB-
CI4JU

## Upgrading

In 2016, the entire line was closed for major engineering
works – itself a good sign, because it means that unlike many
secondary French lines, the Aurillac – Clermont route is not
under threat.

But it did mean that the only trains I saw were stabled in
the now very overgrown sidings next to the station, including
a withdrawn X2200 *autorail*.

However, enough of the station remains for imagination to
envisage how it must have been in its heyday: one of those
places whose geographical context bears little relation to its
operational importance.

Above
**X4039 from Aurillac (09.05) to Saint-Flour–Chaudes-Aigues (11.35) pauses at Neussargues on 29th July 2018.**
Photo: Gwenaël Piérart.

## The model

It has been observed that railway modellers' preference for rural settings does them no favours, since rural railways were able to sprawl to a greater extent than in the cities and towns. This was especially so in rural France, where land was abundant and cheap. So we are again faced with doing justice to a location that is far too large for the average modelling space. But the whole point of this station is that it is (or was) rather grand, and I am loathe to reduce distances more than is absolutely necessary, since this is one of the main give-aways in so much model photography. That said, the main attraction of Neussargues may well be its operational interest, in which case some visual compromise may be of secondary importance.

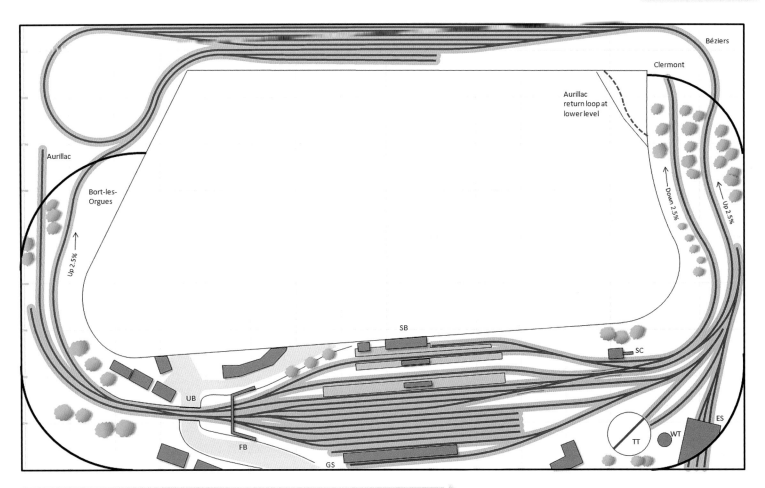

To full scale, the station and approaches would extend to around 6m (20') even in N: this is just not going to fit into a tiny space, so I have assumed a small bedroom or medium shed of 4m x 2.4m as the space needed for a round-the-walls layout. It is just possible, though an extra metre on both dimensions would work wonders.

I have not shown the door, but it would be possible to have a duck-under or lifting flap in several positions.

I model (and plan) in N precisely because one is able to be relatively expansive, and it would be a pity to lose the 'open' nature of the station, which is very typically French.

I am aware of a very fine HO model of the station being built, which has placed it on the diagonal of a room some six metres square, albeit with some compression. This can be seen at

www.trainsdumidi.com/t1493-neussargues-en-ho

Above left
**Looking east. X2800 *autorail* and trailer at the platform.**
Photo: P.Poustache collection.

Far left
**The lowered access section of the platform is clearly marked.**
Photo: Papou Poustache.

Left
**Looking west towards the footbridge.**
Photo: Ian Stock.

Above
**An old postcard view of the road side of the station building.**

Right
**The Société d'Autobus Francolon et Cie. proudly promote their connecting bus services to Chaudesaigues (*sic*) and Pierrefort.**

In order to shorten the station, it is necessary to lose a few of the roads in the marshalling yard, and to curve the approach lines round much more sharply than desirable, but the overall impression will suffice. I have also taken advantage of modern rationalisation to save the length demanded by some pointwork, though some former tracks could probably be put back in if desired. As the track layout has changed several times over the years, I have ended up with a hybrid which, while not 100% accurate, does capture the spirit, and permit all of the main moves. I have assumed the use of Peco track, though custom-built track would of course make it possible to remove some of the compromises, particularly with the scissors crossing at the east end of the station.

The land rises on the side of the station opposite the main buildings, so it is logical to use this as a backdrop to the station itself. At the right hand end of the station (as viewed), the two lines to Aurillac and Bort-les-Orgues can curve away towards their storage sidings, while to the left, the line towards Clermont falls, and that to Béziers climbs sharply above it. If a wider room were available, this section could be extended with some attractive scenic modelling. Both routes ultimately disappear into the trees.

It would be easy enough to complete the line with the normal run to a fiddle yard, but this would mean losing some of the gradients – and I also think that the operational scope requires something a little more complex. So I have envisaged the far side of the room having a narrow, multi-level storage area, with each of the three main approaching routes having its own sidings, ending in return loops in the far corners of the room. Digital electronics are now such that return loops are not the operational problem they once were.

This arrangement allows the Clermont line to fall at around 2.5%, while the Béziers line climbs at the same rate. By the time they reach the storage area, there is enough room between them to accommodate the Aurillac yard coming in from the opposite direction. The branch to Bort-les-Orgues also climbs steeply to reach sidings at the same level

Above
**Z7372 (built 1984), working as TER 15943 *Aubrac* from Neussargues (14.35) to Béziers (19.28), 29th July 2018.**
Below
**The turntable is another relic of the steam era.**
Photos: Gwenaël Piérart.

as the Béziers ones. (I have drawn in the top-level sidings to show the idea; the Clermont storage is identical, but at a lower level, while the Aurillac one is a mirror image at an intermediate level).

As always, choosing a period would be difficult: while the modern era is easier to resource in French N (there are few good steam locomotive models available), the now-rationalised station is probably less attractive than it was in the past. Therefore, I would suggest that the 1990s to 2007, before the use of electric locomotives ceased, would probably be the best.

At that time, the through services were being hauled from Béziers by the vintage BB8600 electrics, with the ubiquitous BB67000 diesels taking over at Neussargues for the run north. Modern X73500 *autorails* were starting to make an appearance, while the older *autorails* remained in evidence, most particularly the classic X2700 *Bleus d'Auvergne*. In more recent times, the X73500s have become the main motive power, though some of the more recent classes such as BB75000 have been seen on the occasional freights that still pass through. In particular, there was a steel coil working to the Arcelor Mittel works at St.Chély-d'Apcher south of St.Flour on the Béziers line as late as 2014. This was double-headed by BB6700s from the Clermont direction, as the 75000s were found to be doing too much damage to the old bullhead rail track (yes, really!) on the line south. This train reversed at Neussargues as the locos ran round, and split the train, taking each half forward in turn.

Below
**SNCF DU 84 RS 9-712 stabled in the yard, 29th July 2018.**
Photo: Gwenaël Piérart.

## Model motive power and rolling stock

French N rolling stock is still somewhat limited, but the main requirements can be met. BB67400s are available from Minitrix, while Rocky Rail provides an excellent BB75500. Arnold and Mabar provide the various *autorails* that would suffice, with more on the way. Piko has a version of the BB25000, which is a dual-voltage version of the 8600, which would be suitably representative. If you want real vintage, there is also the BB8100 from HobbyRail: I am not sure whether they ever worked the line, though some were based at Béziers, so it is not beyond the realm of possibility – and they are splendid. Unfortunately, the Z7300 electric multiple unit stock used on the *Ligne de Causses* local trains is not available.

In terms of 'critical' rolling stock, the obligatory Corail coaches are available, as are steel coil wagons to permit the running of the Arcelor Mittel train.

Were the space available to model Neussargues in HO, then most of the motive power constraints would disappear.

## Conclusion

I think that Neussargues would make a superb model. It may not be the most photogenic of stations – functional is probably the word – but it has quite an attractive setting. And if operation is your thing, there is much to recommend it. The 1,500V catenary would be a challenge all of its own!

**Robert Goyvaerts** models a rural freight transfer facility. *Photographs by the author.*

# The goods shed

The inspiration for this scene was an old postcard which I found on the internet. With just that old image as a guide, the model would be more of an interpretation than an exact representation.

There are enough wooden trusses in my old farmhouse that would serve as an example of the construction, so this aspect would not be a problem to duplicate.

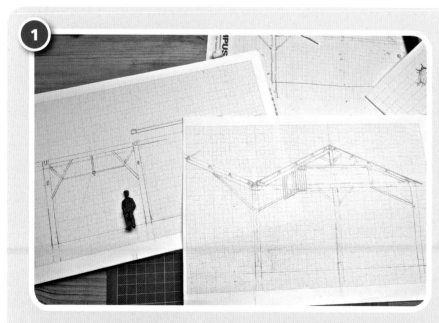

1. Since this is a long-term construction project,
I like to make a sketch, a working drawing,
to be able to work out the right proportions.
The figure serves as a yardstick,
a reference to be able to achieve realistic heights.
Errors in estimation may be made quickly
but are usually only discovered when it is too late.

2. The wooden posts and beams are made of white poplar wood which I had to hand in my workshop and is very suitable for this application.
The visible knots are tiny pieces of walnut dowel (chosen for the colour contrast) which I cut and inserted into holes drilled into the post.

3. The trusses are assembled on a jig to ensure they are identical. Small holes are drilled for the pegs that would in real life hold them together – here the parts are glued.

4. With the trusses, beams, and posts ready, everything can be assembled. The posts are placed on tapered 'stone' pedestals.

5. The pointy planking has been 'nailed' to the beams. A second, decorative, layer has been added on the end of the structure.

6. The overhanging part of the shelter will be situated over the track so goods can be loaded and unloaded without getting wet.

7. The corrugated roof covering is made out of aluminium sheet that has been chemically weathered with ferric chloride – this is effective but not without risks: work outside, protect eyes, hands, and mouth, and have plenty of fresh water to hand in case.

8. After rinsing thoroughly, the individual parts can be glued with ordinary white glue.
I hold them in place whilst setting with lead weights.
All this is done after weathering the wooden structure.

9. The loading dock is made from 2mm thick card and architects board with the paper covering taken off one side.
It is a great imitation of concrete.

10. The bricks that make up the walls of the dock are made of tiny pieces of cut cork. The surface structure of this fine cork is very similar to brick. The work requires patience, but is that not the essence of modelling?

11. When the mortar courses are filled with plaster, they look like the real thing.

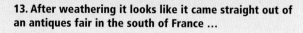

12. The iron gates that once closed the road to the chateau are made of brass rod and strip. The parts were placed on a drawing, held with tape, and soldered together.

13. After weathering it looks like it came straight out of an antiques fair in the south of France …

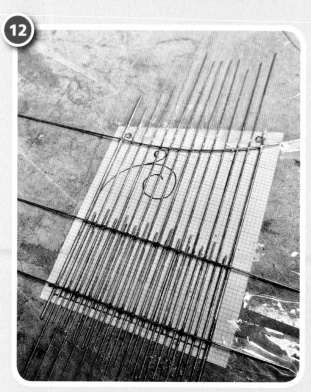

**14. I painted the backdrop according to what I imagined the landscape in the Ardèche would look like. The difficulty is always the transition from three dimensions to two – you must carefully observe colours and perspective.**

To complete the story, a few photographs of the finished scene.

The yellow Petolat tractor was made from a brass kit sold by Loco Diffusion; sadly this company is no longer in business.

Chemins de Fer Départementaux *locotracteur* Y, used on the Vivarais network, was also built from a Loco Diffusion brass kit.

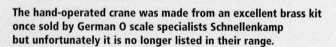

The hand-operated crane was made from an excellent brass kit once sold by German O scale specialists Schnellenkamp but unfortunately it is no longer listed in their range.

The Citroën AMI 6 car and the pre-1969 type H van were acquired cheaply at exhibitions, and subsequently detailed and repainted. I do not remember the makers, and as they are now stuck down …

The shed scene will eventually be placed on my permanent home layout, but before that it has been exhibited as a separate diorama.

*A bientôt, mes amis!*

# Coal in the Cévennes

# Bessèges

## Gregoire Kessedjian
has made an 'animated diorama' in N.

**H**istory
Bessèges is located in the Cévennes region and grew with the development of the coal industry during the beginning of the 19th century. In 1857, the railway linking Bessèges to Alès was inaugurated; the principal aim was the transport of coal. The Compagnie Houillère de Bessèges bought out the Gagnières mining company in 1924 to increase the profitability of the facilities. In 1946, the consolidation of the coal industry lead to the nationalisation of the Houillères du Bassin des Cévennes (Cévennes basin collieries). In parallel, a metallurgical industry was established at Bessèges, on the initiative of the Minister of Armament. Steel tubes were first produced in 1920 and seamless steel tubes in 1921. The steel mills of Bessèges were noted for high quality products and maintained the industrial activities of this region even though coal mining stopped at Bessèges in 1956 and in 1964 for rest of the Cévennes. The steel tube factory remained the only industry, until 1987.

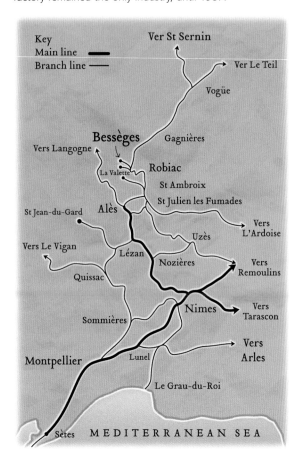

Above
**The industrial side of the site.**
**Only the beginning of the coal plant is reproduced in the model.**
**In the background is the workshop for mine equipment, the old coal washing plant.**
**The CC65500 diesels are by Startrain.**

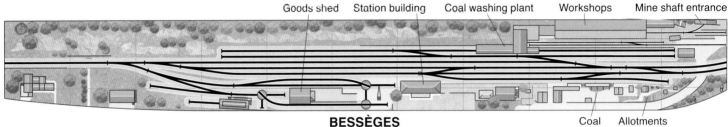

Goods shed   Station building   Coal washing plant   Workshops   Mine shaft entrance

**BESSÈGES**

Overall size: 330cm x 40cm. Each grid square 30cm x 30cm.

Coal   Allotments

## An animated diorama

The idea behind this project was the creation of an 'animated diorama' as a showcase for my rolling stock models. The main difficulty was finding accurate information for the right period as the place had gone through decades of industrial evolution. Old postcards were very important to get the atmosphere of the 1950s.

A central element is of course a plan of the site, which I did not have when I started building the model. Fortunately, the actual location is still undeveloped so a site survey allowed me to reproduce the main buildings.

The visible track had to be an important element, and for me it was impossible to start without wooden sleepers and fine rail; I chose Micro Engineering code 40. The rail is just soldered to copper-clad epoxy sleepers (0.8mm thick printed circuit board) and brass pins, but there are no fine spikes to reproduce the typical French rail fastenings (bolt heads).

The sleepers follow the Paris-Lyon-Méditerranée symmetrical arrangement with sixteen per 12m for main lines and fourteen per 12m for sidings.

The points were all scratchbuilt. They are manually operated by rods, with wooden knobs on the fascia; the electrical feeds are controlled by a switch under the baseboard (moved by the rod).

Classic return loops and storage cassettes are located at either end of the layout. These hidden sections use Peco code 55 track for solidity and ease of construction.

The layout can be operated with either conventional analogue DC (using Gaugemaster units) or DCC.

The framework was made of 10mm plywood in a 'showcase' format complete with lighting to set the scene.

A movable hardboard panel can be placed to enclose the front and protect the layout.

## Motive power and rolling stock

Why an imprecise or idealised period? Partly to disguise a shortage of enough authentic stock. In reality, after the Second World War, the main locomotives which would have been in use were old PLM steamers but as these are not available as models I have to use what can be found – 050A

Top
**Overall view of the layout.**

Right
**The station building was the headquarters of the Compagnie Houillère de Bessèges founded in 1857. The Lyon-Méditerranée company (not yet PLM) were contracted to operate the railway, largely dedicated to coal transport.**

Below left and below
**The station approach follows the real situation, with only a slight factor of compression.**

Below
**X2804 running as the *Cévenol* has been diverted to Bessèges.
The model is by REE/Mikadotrain.**

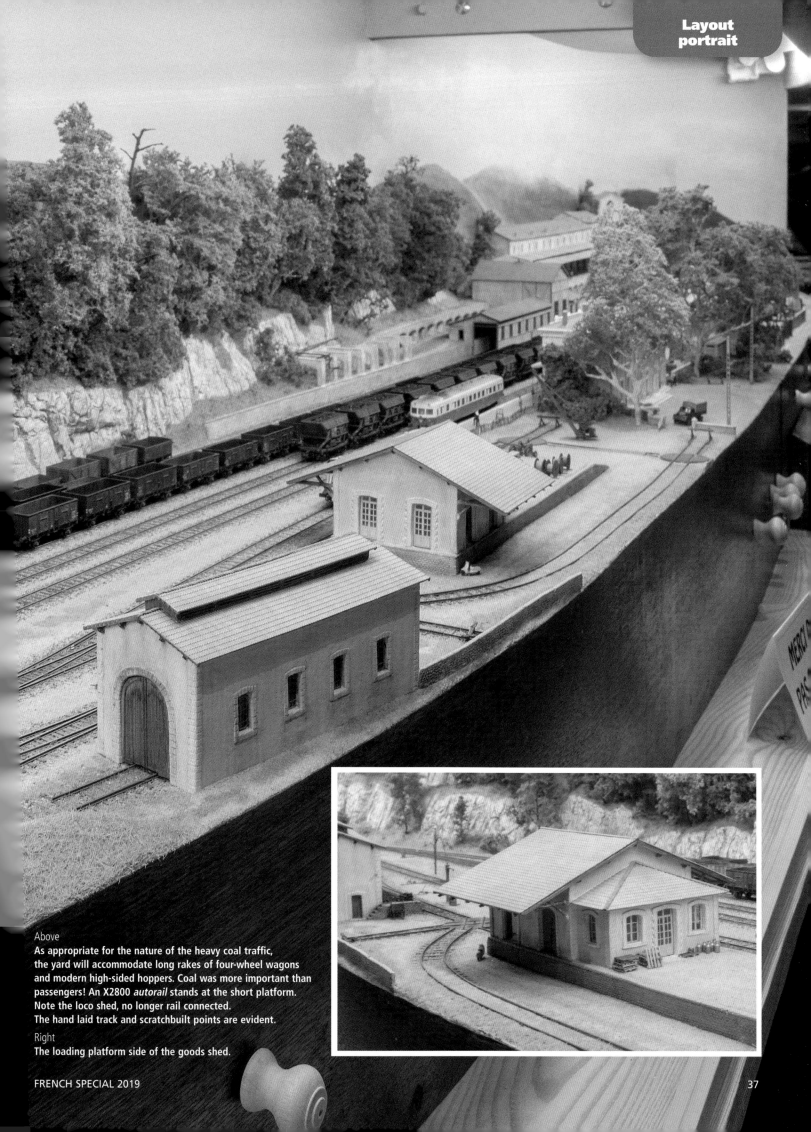

Above

As appropriate for the nature of the heavy coal traffic, the yard will accommodate long rakes of four-wheel wagons and modern high-sided hoppers. Coal was more important than passengers! An X2800 *autorail* stands at the short platform. Note the loco shed, no longer rail connected. The hand laid track and scratchbuilt points are evident.

Right

The loading platform side of the goods shed.

Above
**Several private industries depend on the railway.**
**The local passenger train consists of a BB66000 diesel (Piko)**
**and six-wheel coaches (LS Models).**

Above right
**A former US Army Transportation Corps GE 44-ton switcher**
**(based on a Bachmann model) is active at the mine.**

(built in Austria for the PLM and similar to k.k.St.B. Rh80), 050B (Prussian G10), 140F, and 141R, followed before long by diesels (CC65500, BB63000, BB66000) and *autorails* (X4200 *Panoramique*, X5500).

The fleet of wagons is a fluid combination of old models from French companies and newer products.

Inspired by old postcards, to represent an old rake used by the coal company I modified some Fleischmann German and Graham Farish British four-wheel coal wagons with fine profile wheels and three-link couplings replacing the standard ones, which made them appear much more realistic.

Above
**050 B 70 from Alès depot, an old Prussian G10 0-10-0**
**(a modified Minitrix model).** Photo: author.

Right
**Graham Farish wooden-bodied four-wheel coal wagons,**
**modified with scale couplings and finer wheels.** Photo: author.

## Sources

*Dans le Gard et l'Ardêche: Le Chemin de Fer d'Alais à Bessèges, de Robiac / Voguë / Teil,* Association Terre Cévenole. Nº.10 in the collection.
http://bessegesdautrefois.e-monsite.com
http://gareauxgares.canalblog.com
http://besseges.fr/histoire
https://fr.wikipedia.org/wiki/Bessèges

Below
**The right-hand end of the layout, with the entrance to the mine shaft.**
**The detailed workers' allotment gardens have been transposed to this location for scenic effect.**

Photographs by the editor.

# Rosult

**Patrice Lomprez,** a member of the Association Ferroviaire Sambre Avesnois in Mauberge, has constructed a scene featuring authentic local brick architecture to operate his extensive collection of Nord rolling stock.

Rosult (pronounced 'Rozu'), a through station situated between Orchies and Saint-Amand-les-Eaux, seemed particularly suitable for modelling as its modest facilities hosted comparatively busy traffic.

## Some history

Although the Chemin de Fer du Nord had a link to the mining region via Douai and Somain since 1853, a decree of 11th July 1864 granted a concession for a direct line between Lille and Valenciennes. The location of Rosult station was confirmed by the administration on 5th June 1867 at a place known as Galmont but at some distance from the town centre. The line was opened on 22nd June 1870, but the venture was short-lived as just six years later a ministerial decree confirmed the takeover of operations by the Nord.

Photographs by the editor.

Top
The level crossing at the Lille end of the station.

Above
A mixed goods hauled by 040 DE 1215 waits on track 4, the refuge loop, as an express made up of Nord *Rapide* coaches (by LS Models) with postal and baggage vans at the head hurtles through behind former Nord Pacific 231 E 41.
Alongside the station building, there is a small signal cabin. Across the road from the station there is the station café.

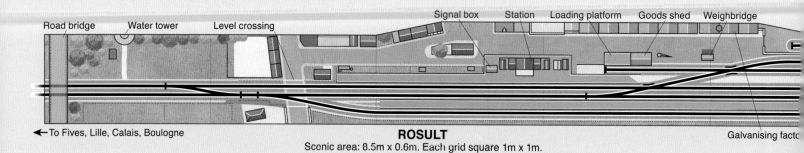

**ROSULT**
Scenic area: 8.5m x 0.6m. Each grid square 1m x 1m.

Road bridge    Water tower    Level crossing    Signal box    Station    Loading platform    Goods shed    Weighbridge

← To Fives, Lille, Calais, Boulogne

Galvanising facto

**Left**
141 R 46 leads a long train of oil tanks from Dunkerque. The concrete road bridge helps to conceal the exit from the storage sidings. There is always a water tower; it also supplies the local domestic network.

**Below**
Two expresses pass at Rosult – 231 K 82 on *Inox* (stainless steel) stock and 231 E 41. The scene looks deeper than 60cm: refuge loop in the foreground, then the running lines, then the railway buildings, and in the background the civil structures (shops, houses, and the factory).

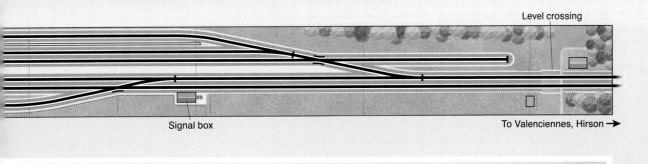

Level crossing

Signal box

To Valenciennes, Hirson →

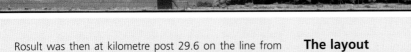

Rosult was then at kilometre post 29.6 on the line from Fives to Hirson, the northern part of the North – East link.

This historical background explains why the architecture of the station building differs from those built or rebuilt by the Nord. The ridge of the roof of the main part of the building is at right angles to the track. Rosult and Raismes-Vicoigne were the only two original Lille – Valenciennes company station buildings to have survived two world wars. After the total demolition of Vicoigne in 1973, Rosult was (for some years) the last remnant of the company. The gradual decline of goods services led to the demolition of the station building in 1994 and the complete removal of all facilities in 1996. Rosult is now classified as a *Point d'Arrêt Non Géré* (PANG), or unstaffed stopping place.

The line was originally single track, and was not doubled until 1920. The layout of the station was not significantly changed: there were sidings and a private connection serving the galvanising factory, and track 4 serving as refuge loop and for separation of local services along the Hirson side.

In 1956, the line was electrified.

## The layout

The period is set at the end of Epoch II/early Epoch III, or more precisely after the creation of the SNCF in 1938 up to electrification in 1956. This period of twenty years or so allows a wide variety of steam locos to be run – 130T, 040T, 050TB, 231E, 231K, 141R, and 150X as well as the first X3800 'Picasso' *autorails*. 150P and 230D steam locos and other standard *autorails* could also be justified.

Passenger stock includes old side door compartment coaches, rakes of Nord *Rapide* and Express coaches, DEV stock, plus Wagons Lits and Pullman cars passing through on prestige services.

There is a large selection of appropriate goods wagons from all the major manufacturers.

The project required several years of research and preparation, consulting archive documents, plans, postcards and the memories of the locals, an aspect of modelling which was interesting both for the creation of the layout and its future operation.

The layout is 10m long and c.4m wide overall, with the scenic section 8.5m by 0.6m at most.

The scenic section consists of seven 1.22m long modules made of plywood, 15mm for the sides and ribs and 8mm for the rest, with integral backscene and top. Each module has a hinged front panel which makes a box to facilitate transport and protects the layout in transit. The three boards with the station, the factory, and the village are 0.6m wide; the other four are only 0.5m wide.

The top incorporates 'cold white' fluorescent tubes, which provide even lighting throughout the scene.

Top
A stopping service for Lille
is provided by an **X4300 EAD**
(*Éléments Automoteurs Doubles*, Dual Self-Propelled)
*autorail* and *remorque* (power car and trailer).

Left
Rosult was equipped with freight facilities appropriate for the level of traffic – goods shed, loading platform with access ramp, and hand-operated crane. Elsewhere in the yard there was a loading gauge and a weighbridge.

At the back, there are four 2.135m boards for the end curves and four long storage loops.

Bolts connect the modules.

A system of wooden legs and bolt-on struts ensures the stability of the layout. The trackbed is 1.2m off the ground.

The visible track is all Peco code 75, with points operated by old post office relays – well suited to this task, and reliable. The storage sidings use Roco code 100 salvaged from older layouts. The minimum radius (behind the scene) is 1m.

The layout is digitally controlled, using a Roco central unit plus a booster and MultiMaus handheld controllers. Lenz LA152 controller connection panels are sited at regular intervals along the fascia to allow control of the trains everywhere on the layout.

Most of the locomotives have sound decoders, which adds to the authentic atmosphere.

## Scenery and structures

The countryside here is essentially flat, so to provide scenic breaks there is a concrete road bridge at the Lille end and a wood at the Valenciennes end.

Above
**230 E (former Prussian P8) 4-6-0 with a train of old compartment coaches.**

Below
**040 D (former Prussian G8) 0-8-0 rumbles through with a block coal train. The galvanising factory has its own private siding behind the brick wall.**

Choosing to model an actual site obliges you to scratch-build a number of the structures. Most were made with shells of mounting card covered with Slater's N scale embossed brick plasticard, which is a better size for HO and looks close to the local style when the mortar joints have been painted and the whole lot weathered.

The layout abounds in cameo scenes and authentic small details, all contributing to the realism of the whole thing. Note the mechanical signalling (LMJ), the kilometre posts,

the edge blocks along the platforms, the sand on the platforms (Anita Décor), the concrete fences (Architecture et Passion), the gardens, the flowers (Heki), the washing hanging on the line, the farm livestock and the wild animals (Preiser), and the road vehicles (Brekina, REE), etc.

## Realism extends to operation

Within the station limits, marked in this period by a sleeper painted white and planted vertically in the ground by the track (not by a *Limite de Manœuvre*, LM, sign), the local goods train arrives from Valenciennes and enters the refuge loop (track 4). After the crossover between tracks 4 and 2 has been set, the train must reverse across onto track 2 and then cross track 1 near the end of the platform before reaching the sidings. This manoeuvre is an interesting aspect of the operation, and provides an alternative to the procession of passing trains. The galvanising factory's private siding can only be accessed by reversing from one of the sidings. To achieve this, the loco must run round the wagons using either the loop siding or track 1, whichever is empty. Usually track 1 is kept free, either for running locos round or holding a slow train – for example block coal trains or trains of oil tanks coming from Dunkerque – so another can overtake – such as fast trains from Calais or Boulogne-sur-Mer via the

Above
**To reach the sidings, local goods trains have to shunt across the running lines.**

Left
**150 X (former German BR50) 2-10-0 runs through Rosult with a mixed goods train.**

Above right
**Another block coal train, hauled by 150 C 661 (former Prussian G12) 2-10-0.**

Right
**The level crossing and wood at the Valenciennes end of the scene.**

Below
**A former PLM Pacific transferred to the north – 231 K 16 and a long train of elegant CIWL stock heading for Lille pass the signal box.**

Lille area. Some expresses, such as the Calais – Basel, pass through Rosult without stopping, at full steam! Sometimes others may be diverted over this route, like the famous *Flèche d'Or* (*Golden Arrow*). Only the workmen's train, often hauled by a tank engine, or *autorails* stop at this station.

A stop signal protects the exit from the station but also allows the sidings to be shunted. Two signal boxes control the points and the mechanical signals. The station has simplified signalling – operation by automatic block. All the other movements are directed by the stationmaster, with his red flag.

The coal merchant does not have a private siding, but must unload from wagons in the station yard.

## Conclusion

At exhibitions, I tend to entrust operation to fellow club members so I can concentrate on talking to the visitors. The period is usually restricted to 1950 – 1956.

But next year the layout will evolve because I plan to change the period, representing the electrification of the line by installing the catenary; this will allow me to runs trains up to 1990 at the latest.

# Marle-sur-Serre

**Jean-Pierre Bout** is a well-known modeller in France and a respected exhibitor. His new layout shows convincingly that O may not need much more space than HO.

This layout was inspired by a single track line in the Aisne department in north-eastern France. In 1907 the Compagnie du Chemin de Fer de Marle à Montcornet opened a 20km connection between the lines from Laon to Hirson and from Laon to Liart, two routes that were operated by the Compagnie du Nord. Passenger services were stopped in 1952 and closure for all traffic followed in 1959.

## Structure

The layout is just over 6m long and 60cm wide, and is made up of two parts. The part with Montcornet depot was started first. In addition to the single track locomotive shed, there is a coal bunker and water tower. Beyond the depot is an unguarded level crossing. This part was shown as a kind of mini-layout at exhibitions in France in 2015.

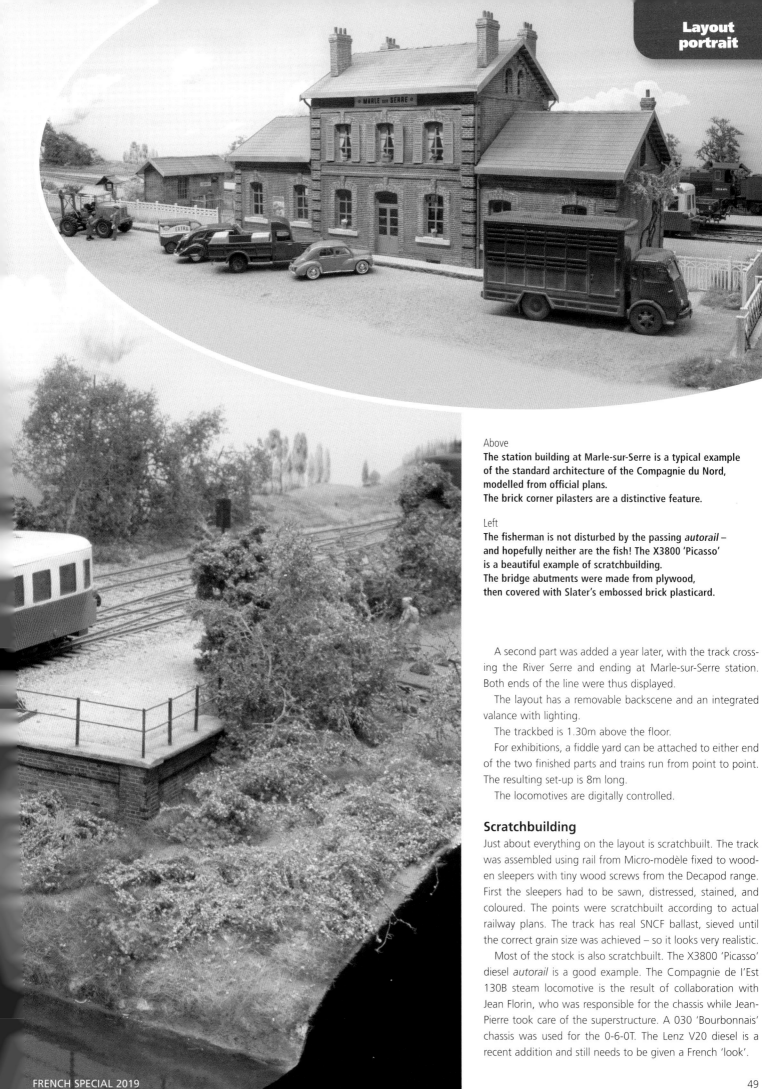

Above
**The station building at Marle-sur-Serre is a typical example of the standard architecture of the Compagnie du Nord, modelled from official plans.**
**The brick corner pilasters are a distinctive feature.**

Left
**The fisherman is not disturbed by the passing *autorail* – and hopefully neither are the fish! The X3800 'Picasso' is a beautiful example of scratchbuilding.**
**The bridge abutments were made from plywood, then covered with Slater's embossed brick plasticard.**

A second part was added a year later, with the track crossing the River Serre and ending at Marle-sur-Serre station. Both ends of the line were thus displayed.

The layout has a removable backscene and an integrated valance with lighting.

The trackbed is 1.30m above the floor.

For exhibitions, a fiddle yard can be attached to either end of the two finished parts and trains run from point to point. The resulting set-up is 8m long.

The locomotives are digitally controlled.

## Scratchbuilding

Just about everything on the layout is scratchbuilt. The track was assembled using rail from Micro-modèle fixed to wooden sleepers with tiny wood screws from the Decapod range. First the sleepers had to be sawn, distressed, stained, and coloured. The points were scratchbuilt according to actual railway plans. The track has real SNCF ballast, sieved until the correct grain size was achieved – so it looks very realistic.

Most of the stock is also scratchbuilt. The X3800 'Picasso' diesel *autorail* is a good example. The Compagnie de l'Est 130B steam locomotive is the result of collaboration with Jean Florin, who was responsible for the chassis while Jean-Pierre took care of the superstructure. A 030 'Bourbonnais' chassis was used for the 0-6-0T. The Lenz V20 diesel is a recent addition and still needs to be given a French 'look'.

Above
Montcornet locomotive shed. Note the very fine wooden fence
between the depot tracks and the main line. This was scratchbuilt,
with the staves cut from 1mm thick veneer, sharpened to a point,
and then washed with various colours to give the appearance
of weathered wood.

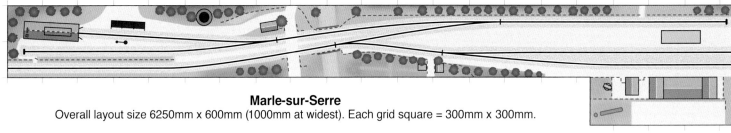

**Marle-sur-Serre**
Overall layout size 6250mm x 600mm (1000mm at widest). Each grid square = 300mm x 300mm.

Left
The depot is in a rural area
and a lane runs alongside
the track, which allows for
some nice detail scenes.
The water tower was also
scratchbuilt.

**The depot has two tracks, and the loco shed on one has a fully detailed interior. Coal is loaded manually – the SNCF used briquettes for firing steam locos. The local fuel supplier brings a barrel of lubricating oil.**

## Buildings

Because the layout represents a real prototype, the buildings also had to be scratchbuilt.

Montcornet loco shed still exists, so the dimensions were determined on the basis of photographs and on site measurements.

The bridge over the river at Barenton-sur-Serre was made from images found on Google Earth, augmented by a site visit to get the correct representation of the steel cladding.

The station of Marle-sur-Serre still exists as a stop on the SNCF line from Laon to Hirson. The station itself, the outside toilet, and the platform shelter were built of brick by the Nord in a style very typical of that company. Jean-Pierre used the plans of the real buildings as the basis for construction, supplemented with his own photos for a number of details.

The buildings are made from Forex (a type of foamboard). First the walls are cut to size, then the window and door openings are cut out. The Forex is then covered with Slater's

**Right**
**In the vicinity of the depot, the sleepers are spaced further apart than on the running line.**
**The point lever comes from the Kit-Zero range.**

**Left**
The ungated level crossing. The whole layout has a self-made backdrop: white and light blue paints were applied progressively, remembering that the sky is lighter at the bottom. Clouds were added later.

**Right**
The X3800 'Picasso' heads for Marle-sur-Serre.

**Below left**
The locomotive is by Lenz, a Deutsche Reichsbahn V20, some of which operated in France; the model still needs a French 'makeover'. The layout is only 60cm wide, but the artistically painted background gives depth, and the river seems to continue behind the bridge.

**Right**
Along the line between the bridge and Marle-sur-Serre station we find allotment gardens, a nice exercise for the modeller with miniature green fingers.

**Below right**
The neighbour is diligently working in her vegetable garden. The garden shed was made of Forex, covered with strips of wood and skilfully weathered.

brick plasticard. The whole is first painted with a red-orange colour, then the mortar joints are picked out in beige. The bricks are then accentuated again with different red and brown shades.

Doors and windows were cut with a Silhouette CraftRobot from a sheet of self-adhesive plastic foil. After cutting, the filigree 'woodwork' is painted and glued onto a sheet of clear plastic glazing. The curtains are hung about 3mm behind the windows. Typical French shutters complete the picture.

The roof covering consists of Redutex sheets.

The result is a beautifully detailed building.

**Above**

A small 030T steam loco is shunting wagons in the yard. The stationmaster's dog is on the alert, as usual.

**Below**

The X3800 'Picasso' *autorail* arrives at Marle-sur-Serre.

**Below**

Next to the station approach a large tree has been felled, and the trunk is about to be dragged away. The road surface is sand, here coloured with pigment.

Photographs by the editor.

**Below**
A busy moment at Marle-sur-Serre station – all tracks are occupied. Dried and sieved sand (collected from a beach in Brittany) was used for the platform surfaces. The stationmaster's wife is hanging the laundry out to dry.

**Above**
Literally the end of the layout. An old rolling barrier protects the entrance to the goods yard (which has not been modelled). On the right is an old Compagnie de L'Est 130B (2-6-0).

# 57 bis rue Eiffefe

Urban freight working
on the *Petite Ceinture*

**François Joyau** has modelled in HO
a section of the inner belt line through part of Paris.

Atter forty years away from the hobby, due to the pressures of professional life, I returned to "little trains" as a result of visiting Rail Expo at the end of 2012.

The design for this micro layout in a showcase was taken from a plan published in *Clés pour le train miniature* in 2013, designed and built by François Fontana and François Fouger. The simple arrangement of a single track line with a passing loop and an industrial siding allowed plenty of operating potential, as at either side there was a hidden yard with three tracks each long enough for a train of 70cm. I adopted it, thinking to continue my first module which had been started the year before.

Below
**Freight traffic dominates in the developing city: steel from the north is urgently needed. The Moyse shunter is by REE, weathered with airbrushed AMF products; the coils are a brass kit from CJ Models. The Y7400 is by LS Models. The working *carré* signal was made from a Rotomagus kit, driven by a servo motor. Houses overlook the track, and suffer the consequences.**

Photographs by the editor.

**Left**
Heavy traffic: an A1A 68000 (Roco) hauling a rake of four-wheel vans direct from the cellars in Burgundy. The weathering was achieved by airbrushing specific AMF products.

**Below**
The district of the three bridges: all different, and made to measure. You can imagine this wooded area is a nice place to live, in the shade of the big trees, with the nearby cinema, the laundry (which leaves the sweet scent of clean linen), and the church at the end of the road, with a weather vane to indicate the prevailing wind. Major extension works are starting on the left. An older couple has just passed under the bridge on the left, starting out on a journey along the cobblestone streets.

The layout is just 2m long, 0.60m wide at the ends and 0.40m in the centre, creating a curved appearance and avoiding straight lines – this gives it a lot of charm. The frame was built from inverted L-girders which slot together using half joints – this gives remarkable rigidity. The backdrop is 3mm MDF glued to the frame, with the sides and the top cover made from cardboard.

The roadbed is glued onto risers fixed to the frame.

The whole scene is lit by alternate warm and cool LED strips. For exhibitions, it has a black cloth which gives a theatre effect. The two 'wings' are painted black and are fixed to the frame with bolts and nuts. Assembly time at an exhibition is usually just one hour, including unloading.

The track (Peco code 75 wooden sleeper) is not placed on a profiled ballast base, except at the exit from the bridge. The rails were painted, then the sleepers weathered with different dry brushing (light grey or black). Three colours of ballast (from ABE) were used, applied loose as usual then fixed with diluted white glue.

I opted for digital control because I had no working equipment left from my previous railway modelling activities. As I therefore had a free of choice of hardware, I invested in a Roco Z21 digital system, which also controls an ESU Switch Pilot that drives the servo motors that operate the Insulfrog points and four mechanical signals.

## Paris encircled

The *Petite Ceinture* or 'small belt' is a double track line which encircled Paris within the city walls; it was built in the time of Napoléon III initially for defence but also to allow Parisians to get around more easily for work or leisure, long before the construction of the Metro underground network.

Under the control of the Paris Lyon Méditerranée, there was a large amount of freight traffic – for example, it was used to supply the wine merchants' premises around Bercy, (where wines from Burgundy, Rhône, Languedoc, and Algeria were delivered), and the abattoirs of La Vilette and Vaugirard.

Passenger traffic collapsed with the growth of the Metro, but freight traffic continued until the 1980s. Some passenger workings, hauled by large diesels, linked the main termini until parts of the line were removed in the late 1980s.

Below

**The large painted sign on the wall is a nod to my friend Christian Navello, a great expert on the two belt lines around Paris. At the foot of this building (a kit by Architecture and Passion) there are two young people chatting alongside a new Solex moped from the 1960s. This is just one of many cameo scenes using figures, all of which have a related story.**

Left
**Tucked in behind the bridges is the art deco Palace cinema.**

Below
**It is difficult to turn the 2CV in the courtyard of the apartment building. Next door a scrap dealer gets anything he can from the attics and cellars of the neighbourhood.**

### My *Petite Ceinture*

To retain the spirit of the design, I decided to keep it single track and I added a short siding and a fuel point.

As the running line is elevated, I had to look for buildings which took this characteristic into account. The belt line stations were almost always at a different level to the tracks, so it only remained to find a station where the tracks were on the upper level. Thanks to members of the *Loco Revue* forum, I was able to find drawings of Vincennes station, and built it from embossed foamboard. The openings were made in heavy coloured card with a Silhouette CraftRobot cutter.

Of course, the dimensions had to be reduced but the essential character was (I hope) retained.

Honouring the Bercy wine area, after extensive research I chose to reproduce the two alleyways that have today become the 'rue de Saint Emilion' and 'the Museum of Patisserie', and the workshop in which *Get* peppermint liqueur was originally made. These buildings are at the heart of the industrial siding.

The siding also accommodates an evocation of the platforms of the slaughterhouse in the rue de Vaugirard, which was the equine abattoir for Paris.

Above
**The Y7400 waits in the loop at Eiffefe station to pass a train in the other direction.**

Below
**The showcase layout: this view makes it look quite large, and hides the simplicity of the track plan.**

The city surrounds the station, and while looking under the bridges we can make out a succession of apartment buildings; the one in the foreground served as a pattern for scratchbuilding all the others. Opposite are three buildings dear to Parisians, including an evocation of the Romainville cinema with its art deco architecture, which is showing a famous French comedy film, *Fanfan la Tulipe,* and a thriller, *Hôtel du Nord.*

The church of Saint Denys la Chapelle is of comparatively simple design so easy to reproduce while being of quite small proportions so it does not dominate the scene.

By the way, it was here that Joan of Arc was baptised before going to drive the English out of France at Orléans, but it was so long ago that the Franco-British friendship will forgive us!

Finally, the Lavoir des Rigollots is based on the public laundry in the rue de Rigolles, in the bohemian district of Menilmontant in the 20th *arrondissement*.

All these structures were scratchbuilt in cardboard, wood, foamboard, and Forex, marked out and cut with the cutter, with window and door frames produced using a Silhouette CraftRobot. They were painted using tube acrylics or artists' oils, applied by the classic foam pad method. They were then weathered with acrylic washes, oil washes, and powders.

And as it needed a signature feature, the typical paved streets of Paris were reproduced by laying the paving stones one by one onto double-sided tape, then painting them, and finally making the joints with powdered earth from the garden, all being secured with diluted white glue.

Lettering for the façades and posters was printed on colourless 'Japan paper' and then fixed with a thin film of diluted white glue.

Above
**A parked Peugeot 404 rusts quietly near the workshop where the famous 'Get 27' peppermint liqueur is made.**

Below
**The intense freight traffic continues its way under the severe eye of the uniformed stationmaster; the white cap was nicknamed 'camembert' by SNCF footplate crews.**

Above

**An evocation of the slaughterhouses in the rue de Vaugirard with its characteristic hopper which threw out the debris and carcasses of slaughtered animals. It was made from drawings based on photographs.**

## Behind the scenes

Two fiddle yards were built initially, according to the original article: one was a turntable, which had the advantage of being able to turn the trains easily without touching the loco, and the other was a sliding plate, which was very quickly abandoned because it was always necessary to handle the locos for each movement, with a high risk of damage.

## In conclusion

With the evolution of computer-based train management techniques, I invested in Train Controller Gold which has enabled, after the construction of a new module and a continuous run behind the scenes in place of the two fiddle yards, realistic automatic operation with sequences of about three quarters of an hour. This allows me to communicate with the public during exhibitions without getting weary.

In addition, the presence of two sector plates driven by stepper motors controlled by Arduino Uno boards, themselves controlled by RailRoad Train Controller, gives a unique aspect to this new arrangement.

Small diesels equipped with digital decoders and 'stay alive' power-packs provide very satisfying shunting sessions.

Below
**In the background, on the left, the wine cellars of the Marquis de la Volière, built from photos and research on site.**

Above

In the foreground, three surviving pre-war structures in the suburbs of Paris.
On the left, a tall, narrow dilapidated house photographed by Didier Lemaitre, converted to scale
by Christian Navello, and modelled in 3D by François Fouger, now available from the Pignon shop
on Shapeways. It was painted with acrylics, and weathered with artists' oil washes.
In the centre, at the back of the yard, a small house where a tramp was squatting.
On the right, the premises of a craftsman cooper, derived from a colourised picture
from the early 20th century of a building located in the district of Montparnasse.

# Industrial scenes

## Goods in the city

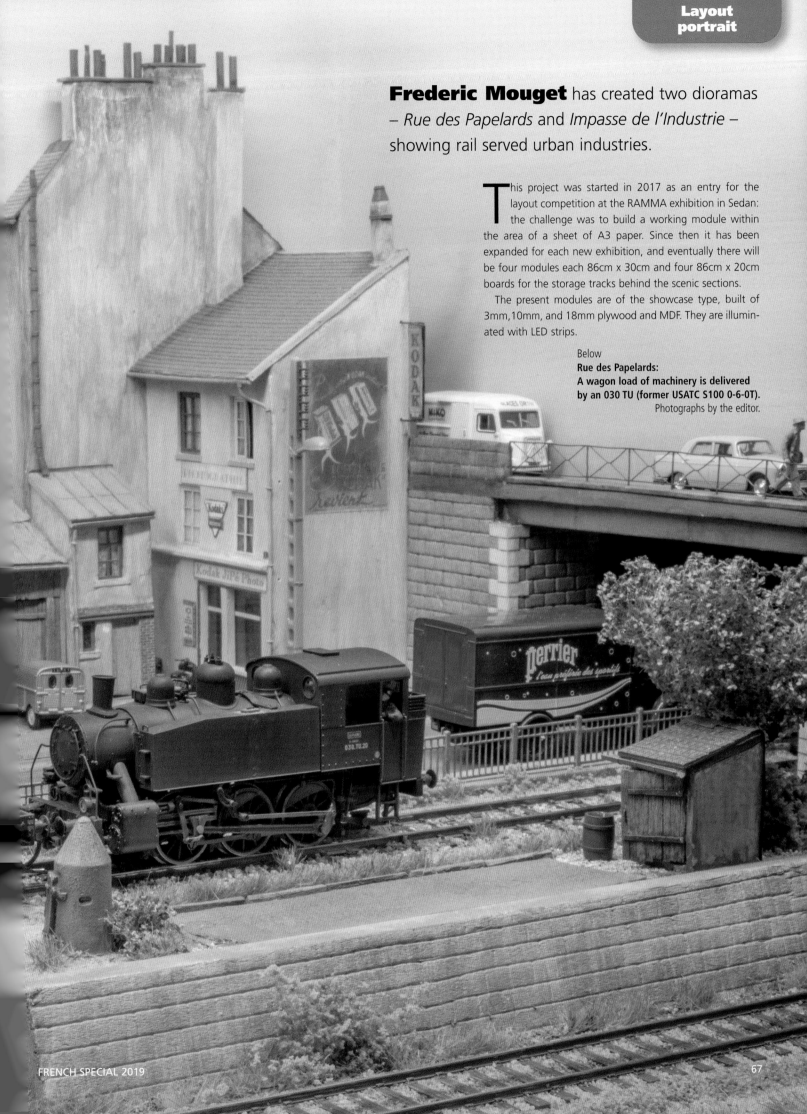

**Frederic Mouget** has created two dioramas – *Rue des Papelards* and *Impasse de l'Industrie* – showing rail served urban industries.

This project was started in 2017 as an entry for the layout competition at the RAMMA exhibition in Sedan: the challenge was to build a working module within the area of a sheet of A3 paper. Since then it has been expanded for each new exhibition, and eventually there will be four modules each 86cm x 30cm and four 86cm x 20cm boards for the storage tracks behind the scenic sections.

The present modules are of the showcase type, built of 3mm,10mm, and 18mm plywood and MDF. They are illuminated with LED strips.

Below
**Rue des Papelards:**
**A wagon load of machinery is delivered**
**by an 030 TU (former USATC S100 0-6-0T).**
Photographs by the editor.

All the buildings are scratchbuilt, mostly with a cardboard sub-structure covered with Redutex textured sheets, embossed plasticard, wood, or paper of various textures, as appropriate. The windows are clear plastic, with the frames cut from self-adhesive paper previously painted the desired colour.

The downpipes are made of solid copper wire, and the chimney pots from the sleeve of the same electric cable.

The road surface and the retaining walls are foamboard, with one side peeled away, the foam scribed, and then painted the required colour.

Track and points are Peco code 75 in the showcase scenes and code 100 for the linking sections and hidden sidings. Every sleepers has been reworked, bevelled, painted, and glued in place, spacing them further apart, before adding ballast (from ABE) and wild grass. Everything was weathered with paint washes, dry brushing, and weathering powders.

Control is currently simple analogue DC but I plan to go digital soon.

Above
**The well stacked dock within the Paper Quick building awaits vans to be loaded.**

The scene is the industrial area of a city somewhere in France in the 1950s – 1960s. It does not represent a real location – the whole thing is purely imaginary, though a few real buildings provided inspiration.

Below
**The rue des Papelards module, with the through track in the foreground.**

## INDUSTRIAL SCENES

Overall scenic dimensions: 198cm x 50cm. Each grid square = 30cm.

Metal fabricators     Paper mill   Book shop   Café   Carpenter

Non-scenic area

**Impasse de L'Industrie**      **Rue des Papelards**

The second module was built specifically to show at the Trainsmania exhibition in May 2019.

Above
Two wagons of scrap parked on the siding
awaiting return to the station.

SSE DE

USTRIE

**Above**
The through track (and the long siding) are at a lower level than the factories.

**Above**
The courtyard of the Bravigou company is rather busy.

Motive power for a famous mountain route

# Old Maurienne locos

**Jacques Poré** introduces the dual system locomotives used on the famous trans-alpine line, and surveys selected HO models.
*Photographs by the author, unless otherwise noted.*

Many fans of old French electric locomotives have a special interest in the machines used on the Maurienne line. These were developed by the Paris Lyon Méditerranée from the 1920s to serve as prototypes for future electrification of the line on the French riviera between Marseilles and Nice. This electrification of the Côte d'Azur did not take place until much later, but the almost 100km of the mountain line from Chambéry to the Italian border at Modane, with its difficult gradients and harsh operating conditions, especially in winter, have been a particular feature of the French rail network for nearly fifty years, notable for the 1,500V DC electricity supply via an outside third rail.

There is a lot of information about the line and its motive power on the website of the Savoyard Association for the Preservation of Railway Material (APMFS) www.apmfs.fr

As unique prototypes and small classes limited to a specific line, the Maurienne machines have not appealed to the major manufacturers but (in HO at least) there have been some very fine models produced by small specialists, the majority of them rather expensive and/or limited editions, it is true, but some are still available or can be found.

My survey of these small series models covers the 'dinosaurs' of the 1920s and the more recent (after the Second World War) machines but is confined to the period when the third rail was still in operation, up to the mid-1970s.

Above
**SNCF 1ABBA1 No.3501, formerly PLM 161 AE 1, at Chambéry depot, 8th September 1962.**
Photo: Walter Boyden, courtesy Frank Hornby.

Below
**1ABBA1 3600 series, made from a kit by Loco-Set-Loisir.**

### The Maurienne 'dinosaurs'

It is easy to talk about the large PLM machines: fortunately Patrick Cassano of Loco Set Loisir (LSL) was interested in the locos built in the 1920s to work freight over the line, and a good twenty years ago he produced kits for all three classes.

The PLM ordered three designs, each consisting of ten machines:

– 1ABBA1 3600 series (SNCF numbering) articulated loco-motives – in fact two single cab units, each of 1A+B wheel arrangement, back-to back and connected to each other.

– 1CC1 3700 series single cab units with end platforms; these were, without doubt, the best looking of the three types.

– 1CC1 3800 series articulated machines consisting of two 1C units back-to-back; with their rounded bonnets, they were undeniably more attractive than the very boxy 3600s.

LSL models were supplied as a complete kits for the mod-eller to build, including all the necessary parts.

Parts are photo-etched brass, with cast brass for large body components as well as a host of small details. If any-thing was missing there was never any problem getting the parts, and LSL were always helpful and ready to advise the modeller about the construction.

I have assembled several LSL kits, and was impressed by the beautiful etching, the level of detail, and the supplied Carmina pantographs (with electric locomotives), always a mark of high quality. The mechanical part was supplied already assembled – with two motor bogies for each of the three machines in question here. Etched number plates and/or transfers were included allowing the modeller to

Top
**1CC1 3800 series, made from a brass kit by Loco-Set-Loisir.**

Above right
**SNCF 1CC1 No.3809, formerly PLM 161 DE 9,
at Chambéry depot, 8th September 1962.**
Photo: Walter Boyden, courtesy Frank Hornby.

Right
**A 1CC1 3800 at Culoz depot in 1976: the end was near.**

reproduce any of the class, and as many as required. They were very nice models, but almost completely unpublicised when they were released and still relatively unknown. I wish that another specialist would take them on now that Patrick Cassano has retired.

As for the appearance, the three LSL models represent the real machines exactly, enabling you to build a fleet of accurate and appropriate Maurienne 'dinosaurs'.

With regard to operation (the mechanism, current collection, traction capability, etc.) the LSL kits for the three Maurienne machines which I have assembled produced quite different results; I tried to understand the differences, in order to improve them.

The 3800 has very good traction over any track layout. The three-axle motor bogies are well balanced and well positioned under the very heavy one-piece body shell, and despite the absence of traction tyres provide great pulling power, even when starting on a 25-per-thousand gradient and curves of 650mm radius as encountered on my layout.

The 3600 has, at first glance, a design quite similar to that of the 3800, but it is noticeably worse on gradients. The explanation is that it actually has a four-wheel powered bogie under one half of the body, and simply a carrier bogie at the other end. In this arrangement, half the weight of the heavy body is on the carrier and as a result the motor bogie tends to struggle on a slope.

The 3700 has the same three-axle bogies as the 3800, but here the photo-etched brass body is too light. It is a good idea to add weights judiciously placed inside the body to improve adhesion. Even with this, my example was still rather weak.

## Passenger locos

The PLM acquired four locomotives for passenger trains, the 2CC2 3400 series. They were the longest single body machines in France, and the most powerful locomotives in the world when they were built.

Two manufacturers have offered them in HO: Bouttuen and, more recently, Lematec. These are exceptional limited edition metal models, beautifully reproduced, with exemplary operation and phenomenal traction power. The Lematec model will run very well on curves of 650mm radius.

All the HO models noted above are equipped with representations of the third rail collector shoes, but of course they are non-functional and will not collect current.

Top
One of the 1CC1 3700 series single units, also made from a brass kit by Loco-Set-Loisir.

Above
2CC2 No.3402 by Lematec. The real 2CC2 3402 has been preserved by the APMFS: it is perfectly presented and can be moved but not under its own power.

Below
At Culoz, a Maurienne BB unit waiting to be scrapped in 1975 or 1976.

## BB 1 – 80 Maurienne

Eleven permanently coupled pairs of the BB 1 to 80 locos were used on the Maurienne line, as well as some individual machines too, though these were not used on the third rail part of the line as the wheelbase was too short to fit the collector.

A good twenty years ago, *Voies Ferrées* published an excellent article illustrated with step-by-step diagrams showing how to transform two Jouef BB series 1 to 80 models into a Maurienne unit, with the two locos connected together by rigid bar. I followed this procedure, from the covers over the roof resistors (scratchbuilt) and the Carmina pantographs to the third rail collector shoes and the earthing poles slung under the sides of the body. The result is a beautiful double machine with very impressive traction power, since it consists of two powered locomotives with traction tyres and significant weight.

More recently, Mistral has also offered a Maurienne BB+BB 1 to 80 unit to modern standards with a choice of two numbers and the option of analogue, digital, or digital with sound. Only one unit is motorised, with the option of having two or four axles of the powered unit with traction tyres, or none – alternative wheelsets are provided, and they are easy to install. The second unit is not motorised. They haul well, especially with one or two axles with tyres. In addition they are well detailed and realistic models.

Top
**In 2016, after a long wait, Mistral released a beautiful double Maurienne unit, consisting of two BB 1 to 80 series units. The model is very detailed, from roof to chassis, and works very well.**

Above
**This BB+BB unit was built from two significantly modified Jouef models.**

Below left
**BB 31 still looking good.**

Below
**BB 75 in Culoz, apparently still in good condition.**

## CC 7100 Maurienne

Although several manufacturers have produced models of the CC 7100, among them Rivarossi, none had offered a true Maurienne version fitted with the third rail pick-up shoes. This changed recently with REE including this variant in their proposals – eagerly awaited.

## CC 6500 Maurienne

Twenty-one of this numerous class (6539 to 6559) were delivered with third rail shoes, in the characteristic green livery with either white or yellow markings.

(They have subsequently carried other liveries, but not in the period when the line was worked by third rail.)

They have been the subject of a number of commercial models.

The first was from Jouef, in the 1970s, as 6551: the model was simplified, as common at the time, but satisfied thousands of enthusiasts for years. Jouef completely revised the model in the 1990s.

More recently, Roco has added the CC 6500 to its range; among the versions is one in Maurienne green.

Among limited edition producers, Gérard-TAB, one of the top craftsmen producing French models from the 1960s to the 1980s, offered several versions of the Maurienne CC 6500; these were exceptional models.

Just a few years ago, Lematec rolled out the entire series of CC 6500 (and CC 21000), including several in Maurienne green, among them one equipped with third rail shoes.

So the CC 6500 'family' is undoubtedly the class used on the Maurienne line which has been the subject of the greatest number of HO products. It is also the only Maurienne type which has been made in other scales, with some in N and O – but all even rarer than some of the HO models mentioned above! O gauge examples have come from AMJL and Lematec; they are museum quality, and have considerable presence.

HO mini scene just 48cm x 42cm for a shelf

# Douce Provence

**Davide Raseni** captures the essence of the south of France in the 1960s.
*Photographs by the author.*

During 2017 I made a small scene to accommodate my favourite German models on a base just 48cm square (see CM February 2018). A year later, when I had enough space in a showcase in my dining room, I thought of making another diorama on a base of about the same size. This time I decided to go to France, due to my love for large SNCF diesels, of which I have several different models.

## The idea

On such a small baseboard this time I chose to make a section of a non-electrified double track line, a classic French situation. As usual, over the years I prepared in advance a box with a lot of commercial accessories for a future French HO diorama. When I was ready to start on this little project, all these elements were enough to give the right setting.

## The structure

As usual I used a rectangular base and side walls shaped to follow the landscape profile made of 8mm plywood.

The double track line is raised by 3.5cm on a foam base at the front, to create a slight slope.

The whole structure was covered with sheets of toilet paper drenched with watered-down glue – very simple and very fast.

**Below**
**The first batch of the class BB67000 was soon dedicated to freight service.
A train of refrigerator vans is hauled by BB67011.**

## The accessories and the setting

Two old but very good plastic kits, three telegraph poles, some cars, and some rows of lavender were the elements I needed to set my little diorama in the south of France.

Because the cultivation of lavender is a classic sight in the south of the country, I decided to put the colourful rows (using Noch products) in the front of the diorama, to emphasise this element. The slight slope improves a landscape which would otherwise be too flat, and allowed me to make a much more interesting scene with a road that climbs to the level crossing.

The diorama is set in Epoch III. For this reason I used wooden sleeper track (Peco code 75 flexible track), some typical French wooden telegraph poles (an excellent brass product by the Italian producer MS Accessori Ferroviari), a classic SNCF level crossing with sliding barriers (an old MKD kit), not automated but attended by a crossing keeper, and a lavender shop together with the owner's private home (an old MKD kit for a bank or post office, but modified).

Above
**Far from the *Tour de France*, a relaxed postman descends a slight slope on his bicycle during his morning delivery round. Behind him an SNCF diesel *autorail* passes the level crossing.**

Right
**A rake of long distance stainless steel (*inox*) coaches hauled by a new CC72000 in its first years of service, running at speed through the fields of lavender.**

Below right
**A BB67000 running light passes an ABJ4 near the level crossing, illuminated by the late afternoon sun.**

Below
**A rusty 141R is hauled to the scrapyard. The steam loco is an old Rivarossi model, heavily weathered with airbrush and powders. The connecting rods have been dismantled, as usual for such transfers, the chimney is closed with a metal cap, and the empty tender is covered with a blue plastic sheet. The final touch is an *adieu* that an unknown hand has chalked on the side of the tender ...**

I have used some classic French cars from the 1960s – such as Citroën, Peugeot, and Renault; as always, the vehicles help to give the scene a very important aspect and define the period.

## The models

I was always fascinated by the large French diesels in two-tone blue livery with white stripes and the old SNCF logo (the so-called Arzens design). For this diorama I have used Jouef, REE Modèles, and Roco locomotives in their first versions, as delivered or in their early years of service. It may be that not all these classes were used in southern France, but I hope readers will forgive me.

The only steam loco featured is an old Rivarossi model of a class 141R; this had been damaged so I modified it slightly more to represent a wreck. I wanted to create a romantic scene with a train made up of a steam loco being hauled to the scrapyard by a modern diesel. So I worked some days on this model with a good result.

Below left
**The kitchen garden of the level crossing keeper's house, with an old woman busy among the vegetables.**

Left
A dramatic view of BB67011 with a long mixed freight running on the wrong line: I imagine that we are still within the station limits and the train has just started from the freight yard and has to work over a short part of the main line in the wrong direction before it reaches a crossover.

Right
SNCF diesels of the 1960s are fascinating – the smart two-tone blue livery with white stripes, the front full of chrome, and the unmistakable side grilles make them unique. Here A1AA1A68020 is running light on a test run, in pristine condition only a few days after delivery.

Below
The essence of railways in southern France during the 1960s: a sunny day with a blue sky, a field of lavender, the chirps of cicadas, and a Renault ABJ4 *autorail* (Electrotren) in its elegant red and cream livery accelerating away after a stop at the station.

VENTE DIRECTE
LAVANDE

Right
The level crossing keeper has closed the gates
a few minutes before the passing of a Renault ABJ4 autorail.
The driver sounds the horn during the low speed passage.

Below right
A touch of sentimentality: BB66117 hauls a withdrawn 141R
off to the scrapyard.

Left
The back garden of the lavender shop with the owners at work.
All the details are products from Noch, Heki, and Faller.

Below
The other building on the diorama.
This old but good MKD kit for a bank or post office
was modified into a private house with shop annexed,
and improved with a lot of details.

The diesel *autorails*, passenger coaches, and freight wagons were kindly loaned to me by my friend Max Di Biagio who has an impressive collection of HO rolling stock.

Many of the freight vehicles and some of the locomotives were slightly weathered with airbrush and powders.

## The photos

This little diorama was made with the idea of taking a large number of different pictures despite its small size. I waited for a sunny day and took it outdoors. The temperature was not helpful but the strong sunlight gave the right atmosphere, just like that of a hot summer in Provence; you will have to imagine the chirping of cicadas and the scent of lavender. Actually, as a joke, I poured some drops of essence of lavender on the row of bushes with an interesting result – the first example of a fragrant diorama!

Below
In the absence of rail traffic, cars are carefully crossing the line.

VENTE DE LAVANDE

# A town with a metre gauge tramway

# Ville en Provence

**Christophe Saclet** has recreated a slice of a small town in Provence in HO.

Below
What would Provence be without its markets?
The plane trees provide the population with a little shade.
The trees are the products of a small specialist supplier.
The figures are from several different packs by Preiser
and Noch, selected and arranged according to their attitude.

**Christophe Saclet** has recreated a slice of a small town in Provence in HO.

Above
All buildings have shutters made of laser-cut cardboard.
This technique was also used for the pharmacy sign.

Above
The advertisement was printed on paper which was then glued
to the cardboard wall. The right-hand part was hand painted.
Several light passes of sandpaper weathered the result.

**Above**
The road by the tram depot has a camber; to achieve this, a strip of Evergreen styrene was glued in the middle underneath.
This is the south of France, so there must be a game of *petanque*! But the employees play after work, of course!

**Left**
The gendarmerie is a copy of the one at St.Tropez. Google Street View allowed me to make a drawing of the façade without actually going there, and the national *cadastre* (the public register defining the area and value of real estate for the purpose of establishing property tax) has a website which allowed me to find the precise dimensions of the frontage.

**Below**
The frame of the shed was laser-cut in cardboard by a specialist craftsman who works to order.

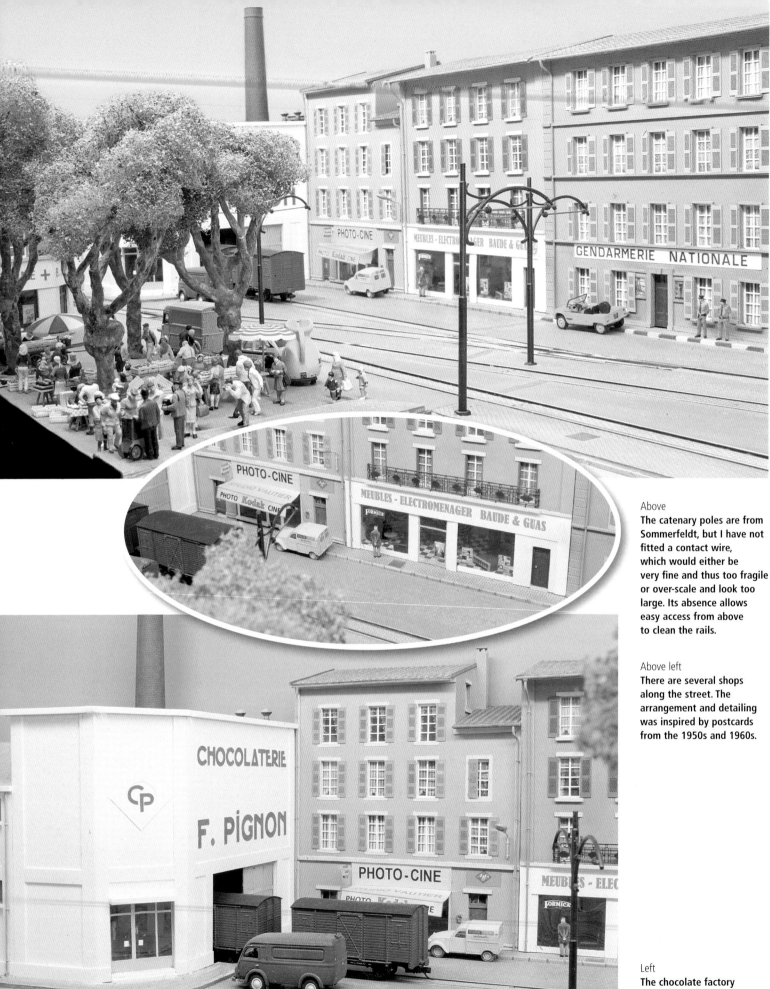

**Above**
The catenary poles are from Sommerfeldt, but I have not fitted a contact wire, which would either be very fine and thus too fragile or over-scale and look too large. Its absence allows easy access from above to clean the rails.

**Above left**
There are several shops along the street. The arrangement and detailing was inspired by postcards from the 1950s and 1960s.

**Left**
The chocolate factory justifies the operation of freight trains. The design was inspired by a real building from the 1930s which was in fact a laundry.

Above

The newsagent's shop is an exact reproduction of a postcard.
Although they are almost invisible,
all the covers of the magazines are correct for the period!
Two businessmen emerge from the hotel and hail a taxi ...

Below

... which is conveniently just passing the cinema.
The authentic period posters advertise two comic films.

Above
The town may be small
but it has a service station
and garage. The interior is
decorated with posters
from the 1950s and 1960s,
not to mention the calendar
with a pin-up!

Photographs by the editor.

Train du Pays Cathare et du Fenouillèdes

# Le train rouge

**Michael Sanderson** discovered a typical French tourist line.
*Photographs by the author.*

I stumbled on the Train du Pays Cathare et du Fenouillèdes (TPCF), which markets itself as *Le Train Rouge*, almost by accident, whilst planning a trip to the more famous *Train Jaune* line in the French Pyrenees. I am very glad I did, as this railway offers some very interesting rolling stock from which to take in the area's fantastic scenery.

As a tourist railway the TPCF is a concept not really seen in standard gauge preservation in the UK. While the railway is operated by a society, the stock is not kept in period condition but painted in the line's own colours and in many cases specially adapted for the tourist market.

The line runs from Rivesaltes, where a connection is made with the SNCF line along the Mediterranean coast, to Axat in the Aude valley. Previously part of the line from Rivesaltes

to Carcassonne, the section from Carcassonne to Quillan retains its SNCF service but the section between Quillan and Rivesaltes first lost its passenger service during the Second World War and then closed altogether in the 1990s. In 1992 an association was formed to re-open the line as far as Axat, and this aim was achieved in the first years of the 21st century.

The line's southern terminus is within the SNCF station where the TPCF have a separate booking office in the main station building. TPCF trains leave from the northern platform.

On arriving at Rivesaltes I found 'Caravelle' unit X4573+ XR8592 waiting on platform 4 ready for the journey as far St.Paul de Fenouillet, where the open stock would be waiting for the trip up second half of the line.

Below
**The station at Rivesaltes with AGC Z27902 in Region Languedoc-Roussillon livery on the main line. The TPCF train can be seen at the far platform.**

**Above**
'Caravelle' *autorail* X4573 and trailer XR8592 loading passengers at Rivesaltes ready for the trip to Axat.

**Right**
**At St.Paul de Fenouillet passengers change to a panoramic train with open coaches converted from freight wagons.**

**Below**
The line runs through the picturesque Aude river gorge.

**Right**
Open coaches provide a fantastic way to view the scenery.
The trains stop for a while on most of the bridges
for passengers to take photographs.

**Below**
The booking office for the TPCF at Axat is located
in a modern extension to the original station.
This also houses the waiting room and gift shop.

**Below right**
At many of the villages along the route
the former station buildings are no longer used by the railway.
Instead shelters have been created in very modern style
with a fabric cover stretched between four metal posts.

Above
**The TPCF logo and livery are seen to good effect on BB63240 as it runs round the train at Axat. Note the bullhead rail track, and the wider sleeper spacing in the sidings.**

Right
**In the yard at Axat station was a second short rake of coaches used on the upper section, also converted from freight stock.**

The first part of the journey runs through vineyards and olive groves and the picturesque towns of Estagel and Maury. The train stops on bridges over the river Agly to allow the passengers to take pictures while the 16th century hermitage of Notre-Dame-de-Pene can be viewed on a hill overlooking the line.

At St.Paul de Fenouillet we changed from the 'Caravelle' to the line's main attraction, a scenic train pulled by BB63240. It was formed of two open coaches converted from K-50 freight wagons and a semi-open bogie vehicle which was formerly an R-91 wagon.

As the train pulls away from St.Paul there is an interesting sight. In a compound to the left a narrow gauge railway is visible which seems to use converted tractors as motive power. The line takes the form of two short ovals of track one inside the other.

The TPCF continues to climb through agricultural land until the scenery becomes more wooded in character after Caudiès-de-Fenouillèdes. The summit of the line, 514 metres above sea level, is reached following a short stop at Lapradelle. From here the track becomes more sinuous in nature, with several bridges and tunnels as we approach Axat. Emerging from one of the tunnels, Axat station can be seen below on the other side of the valley.

Right
The TPCF bought this T2 sleeping car with the aim of creating railway-based holiday accommodation at either Axat or Lapradelle.

**Above**
'Caravelle' X4554+XR8564 was converted to a luxury train
by French Rail Cruises as part of an attempt
to tap into the high end tourist market.
Acquired by the TPCF in 2009, it is now available for charters.

**Left**
Passenger services on the revived TPCF were inaugurated
by 'Picasso' *autorail* X3944. This is now undergoing restoration.
Seen from the train at Caudiès-de-Fenouillèdes.

**Right**
One of the semi-open coaches. This was converted from
an R-91 wagon and has space for 87 passengers.

**Below**
The wagon ancestry of the open coaches is clearly visible.

On arrival at Axat we travel through the station past sidings where stock is stored and continue on 2km through the spectacular gorges of the Aude to St.Martin-Lys. Here the line finishes rather abruptly at a makeshift station by a factory. The train does not wait for long here but returns to Axat where there is a break before the return to Rivesaltes.

Trains run from April to the end of October, with the open stock being used from June to September.

The tourist nature of the line with its bespoke livery and coaches could make an appealing modelling project. The modern waiting shelters seen at some of the intermediate stations would be a particularly interesting feature. A free-lance model would allow the modeller to use their own livery and to mix items of stock not usually seen together.

# Bard-Daizamy

The latest industrial narrow gauge creation in O-14
from the **Escadrille Saint Michel**
is designed to be viewed from all sides.

Layouts built by members of the French modelling club Escadrille Saint Michel have regularly appeared in CM. At the OntraXS! model train exhibition in the Dutch national railway museum in Utrecht in March 2019 they unveiled their latest creation, as usual an industrial narrow gauge theme with interesting operation.

The theme is traditional, transporting coal from loading to unloading. On the other hand, it is impossible to determine exactly where this place is located. It is a mixture of constructions inspired by typical European and American industrial sites. Normally these two styles cannot coexist, so purists may cry scandal. But such installations have common features, and the trick is to create a convincing combination. Welcome to the miniature world of ESM!

## Every layout tells a story

We are on a coal mining site. The activity is not intense because it is small local production. There is no road access, and the only transport is by 60cm gauge railway.

The loading site occupies a small area. It is very minimalist – there are only two tracks, one dedicated to loading and the other for stabling an empty train.

There is just enough space for a skip full of scrap and an old bulldozer. Two workers are having a discussion near an old generator that supplies power to the site.

After crushing the coal goes down into a storage bin using chutes – no need for a mechanism, gravity does the work. A conveyor belt transports the coal from the storage bin to a hopper under which there is a train of five wagons. There is no hurry, the speed of loading is not very fast. This is undoubtedly the ideal place to apologise for slowness. The driver must be very careful to stop precisely under the hopper. It is also imperative not to have a load that exceeds the top of the wagon, otherwise there may be problems when it comes to unloading. When all five wagons are full, the train is ready to go.

**Below**
**The loading point. There is little space but all the facilities needed to load the coal.**
**A train of empty wagons is parked on the siding.**

Photographs by the editor.

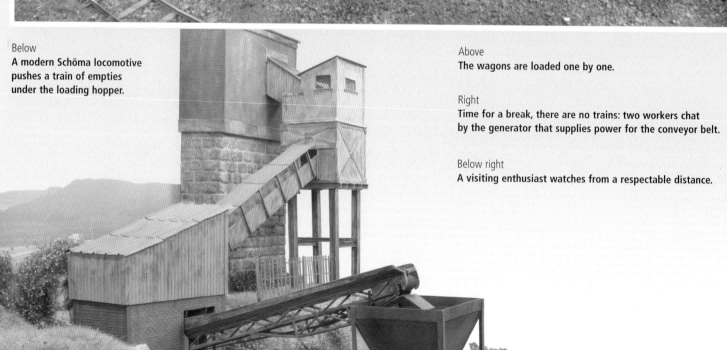

**Below**
A modern Schöma locomotive
pushes a train of empties
under the loading hopper.

**Above**
The wagons are loaded one by one.

**Right**
Time for a break, there are no trains: two workers chat
by the generator that supplies power for the conveyor belt.

**Below right**
A visiting enthusiast watches from a respectable distance.

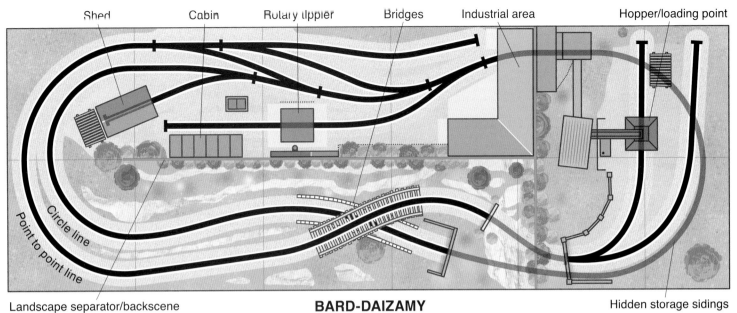

Shed    Cabin    Rotary tipper    Bridges    Industrial area    Hopper/loading point

Circle line

Point to point line

Landscape separator/backscene

Hidden storage sidings

**BARD-DAIZAMY**
Overall size: 170cm x 60cm. Each grid square 30cm x 30cm.

The line first passes through a short tunnel under a hill, then it crosses a small ravine on a wooden bridge. The peculiarity of this wooden bridge is that it goes over another brick bridge on which there is another line. The two come together some way further on. The civil engineers needed a lot of skill when surveying the route. The track is on such a gradient because the unloading site is below the point of extraction; it takes good brakes to slow the train.

It is a period of drought, the grass has a pale green hue. This is in contrast to shrubs and trees that have a brighter colour.

Eventually the train arrives at the terminus. There is a shed for repairing wagons and locomotives. The administration offices are in the brick building, while the wooden construction is the workers' locker room.

To empty the wagons, the company chose gravity unloading. Each wagon goes through a rotary tipper. It is a simple but effective system.

Of course, this is a totally imaginary situation, another vision of an ideal world created by ESM. (It has been suggested that these three initials stand for 'Extraordinary Stuff Miniaturised'!)

### The layout

The group always works in 1:43.5 scale, representing the 60cm track with accurate 14mm gauge. As usual, all the track and turnouts are handmade.

The concept of this layout was borrowed from a French modeller who had himself copied a Dutch modelmaker. For the sake of discretion, we will not mention the names! But the track plan was slightly modified and re-arranged to suit.

The layout is not very large, at just 1.70m x 0.60m, but it has one particularly unusual feature – it is designed to be viewed from all four sides, which makes it seem much larger. Naturally it was built for exhibiting, and with presentation in mind there is a centrally supported valance with integrated LED lighting.

There are two circuits, on two levels.

One line is point to point. An empty train leaves the unloading area, pushing the wagons up the hill to the loading hopper. The return is, of course, with the loaded wagons.

The other line is a continuous circuit that also leaves the unloading area but descends behind the scenes, hidden under the loading area, and then returns to its starting point.

There are three zones separated by two scenic dividers. The first defines the loading area, the second separates the unloading point from the landscape section with the bridges. These scenic dividers are very useful, allowing us to mix different scenery within relatively little space.

Inset
A Diema DS 40 leaving the tunnel, about to cross the wooden bridge.

Above
Two trains passing. The difference in level between the two tracks is clear. The landscape is tortuous: after leaving the tunnel there is a tight curve then immediately the line crosses a wooden bridge. The right hand track climbs to the loading point, the left line descends to the hidden storage sidings.

Above
**The unloading installation is very basic.**

Below
**There is a small shed for the maintenance of locos and wagons.**

## The loading area

The upper part of the layout features the loading area. The conveyor belt was made from an old Faller HO kit (ref.B195) which is perfect for loading O scale Hudson wagons. Of course, we have made it functional: the original constant speed AC motor was changed for a DC motor so we can adjust the speed of the conveyor belt with a conventional controller.

Apart from the conveyor belt and the bulldozer, all the structures and scenery were scratchbuilt.

The entrance to the tunnel and the wooden retaining wall were made of ice cream sticks. (Modelling is a good excuse to eat a lot of ice cream!)

The chutes and hoppers are made from various Evergreen styrene sections.

The stone wall is expanded polystyrene.

## The landscape area

The mountainous landscape is rather complicated. The challenge was to get two tracks crossing on different levels with two bridges and two tunnel entrances in a small space. We think it is successful and convincing, and brings an original touch to the layout.

The wooden bridge was built with candy floss sticks.

The brick bridge has a wooden base covered with Redutex self-adhesive textured brick sheet.

The rocks are carved plaster.

*Above left and above*
**A wooden bridge over a brick bridge!
The engineers who built the line
must have had nightmares!
How to cross two lines on different levels
in so little space. There are also two tunnels,
as the lines have to pass through the hill.**

*Below*
**The industrial unloading area
(on the left) is quite a contrast
to the landscape area
which is closer to nature.**

Above
**The company administration building straddles the line.**

Above right
**A workman can be seen through the window of the wooden hut, but he does not seem motivated to work.**

## The unloading area

On the lower part of the layout, a rotary tippler is used to empty the wagons. There is no high technology – the control is manual, done with a simple crank and Meccano gears.

Using a rotary tippler did pose one significant question: how to turn each loaded wagon individually without uncoupling it from the others? We found a trick that works very well – just use small fishing hook swivels.

## Scenery

Foliage of various kinds is from the usual brands, well known to modellers. Use of a Noch Grasmaster to apply the synthetic grass fibres guarantees that they will stand vertically – it is a very satisfactory effect. Spruce and larch trees are from Model Scene. The soil is just stained sand.

The buildings were weathered with Vallejo acrylic paints and dry coloured earth powders.

**Left**
**The wagons are unloaded slowly one by one using a rotary tippler. The rusty roof would not provide much protection from the rain.**

**Below**
**Brick, wood, and coal – three typical elements which give an industrial atmosphere to this place.**

## Stock

We now have quite a collection of different industrial narrow gauge locomotives which may be used on the layout. Typically you will see a Gmeinder (made from a Gecomodel kit), a Diema DS 40 (a kit by Trains d'Antan), and a Schöma (scratchbuilt).

The wagons were all made from KB Scale kits.

## Conclusion

This relatively small but well detailed layout, with a proper purpose to the operation and some interesting working features, seems to have pleased visitors to exhibitions so far – not to mention its designers and builders.

As usual, the layout name is another terrible pun, derived from *Bar des Amis*, or in English 'Friends Bar'.

An undergound railway takes us far back in time

# Pimbelles Carhye

**Isabelle Voynet** has modelled
an unusual tourist line.

It is aboard a small train that we are able to visit the caves of Pimbelles Carhye. The setting is completely imaginary, but inspired by places that really exist, such as the caves of Rouffignac or Lacave, which house prehistoric paintings and numerous rock formations.

## A typical visit

After passing through the ticket office, a tiny wooden building at the entrance of the site, visitors discover the reconstruction of a nomadic settlement of the paleolithic era. They may also witness a flint making demonstration by an archaeologist.

Then they can take a seat aboard two open 'toast-rack' coaches, hauled by a Gmeinder locomotive. This was a diesel, recovered from a brickyard, and has been converted into a battery electric vehicle so as not to pollute the interior of the caves.

The train enters the cave through a reinforced security door. Spotlights light up along its way to illuminate the walls which are adorned with rock paintings which show mammoths, aurochs, deer, horses, and hand prints in outline. On the ground, you can see some footprints left by our distant ancestors.

The train then plunges even further into the bowels of the earth to reach the second part of the cave. The visitors continue on foot between the stalactites and stalagmites, and end in a cave where they can see unusual rock passageways

and gours, a type of formation in the form of a stone dam, with rimstones made up of calcite and other minerals that build up in cave pools. The formation looks like stairs, and often extends into flowstone above or below the original rimstone.

Meanwhile, in the forest above the cave, a couple are having a picnic and some hikers enjoy a walk on the trail on this sunny autumn day; maybe they will be able to see some of the wild animals.

At the end of the day, after the last run taking visitors through the caves, the locomotive is driven to the shed for maintenance and recharging, and the guides have a rest with a coffee in their small office.

*Above and left*
**The train shed, the reconstructed prehistoric camp, and the ticket office.**

*Photographs by the editor.*

## PIMBELLES CARHYE
### Overall size: 145cm x 35cm.

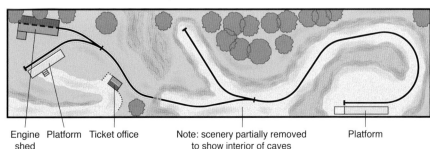

Engine shed  Platform  Ticket office    Note: scenery partially removed to show interior of caves    Platform

Above
**An overall view of the layout.**

## The technical side

The layout occupies an area of just 145cm x 35cm. The structure is made of plywood.

The rolling stock comes from the Busch *Feldbahn* range. The 6.5mm gauge track has a metal band under the sleepers, and the loco is equipped with a powerful magnet which holds it to the rails to increase its adhesion and improve electrical contact. Control is analogue. The system comes with a simple battery power pack/controller, but a mains adaptor is available.

When I started the project, only diesel locomotives were produced, so I imagined the Gmeinder had been converted for underground use. Now Busch offer models of genuine battery electric mine locomotives.

I scratchbuilt the bodies of the open coaches on Busch underframes.

## Scenery

With the exception of some components from kits (such as benches, barriers, and spotlights), I scratchbuilt everything.

The rock faces are expanded polystyrene, covered with a mixture of plaster and cellulose powder and coloured with acrylic washes, pastels, and scenic ground cover.

The stalactites and stalagmites were made with the same mixture, applied on various supports – such as cocktail sticks, brass rods, etc., and some produced by 3D-printing. I also included some natural elements.

The ground cover consists of soil from the garden, mixed tree leaves, and various flock materials, with static grass fibres applied electrostatically.

The trees come from various specialist craft suppliers (such as Arboris Miniature, Sylvia SDD, and Anita Décor), and some were home-made from sea foam covered with foliage materials.

The plants were painted using pastels.

The buildings are wooden, and fully furnished inside; I tried to put in the maximum amount of detail. The doors of the shed are functional.

I dressed the prehistoric figures in the skins of animals made from tissue paper, and equipped them with tools of real flint or wood.

The spotlights are controlled manually, following the progress of the train.

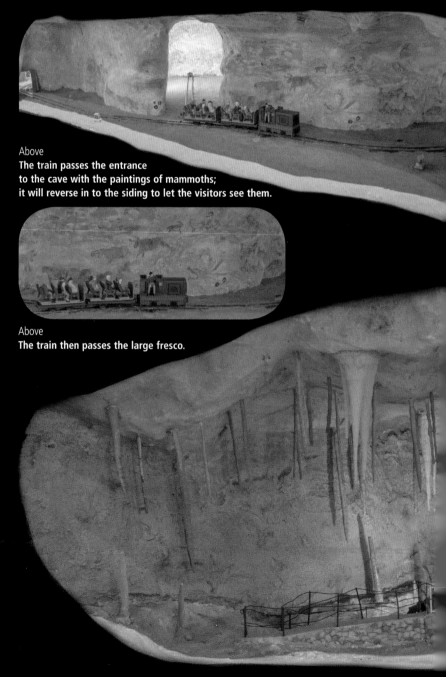

Above
**The train passes the entrance
to the cave with the paintings of mammoths;
it will reverse in to the siding to let the visitors see them.**

Above
**The train then passes the large fresco.**

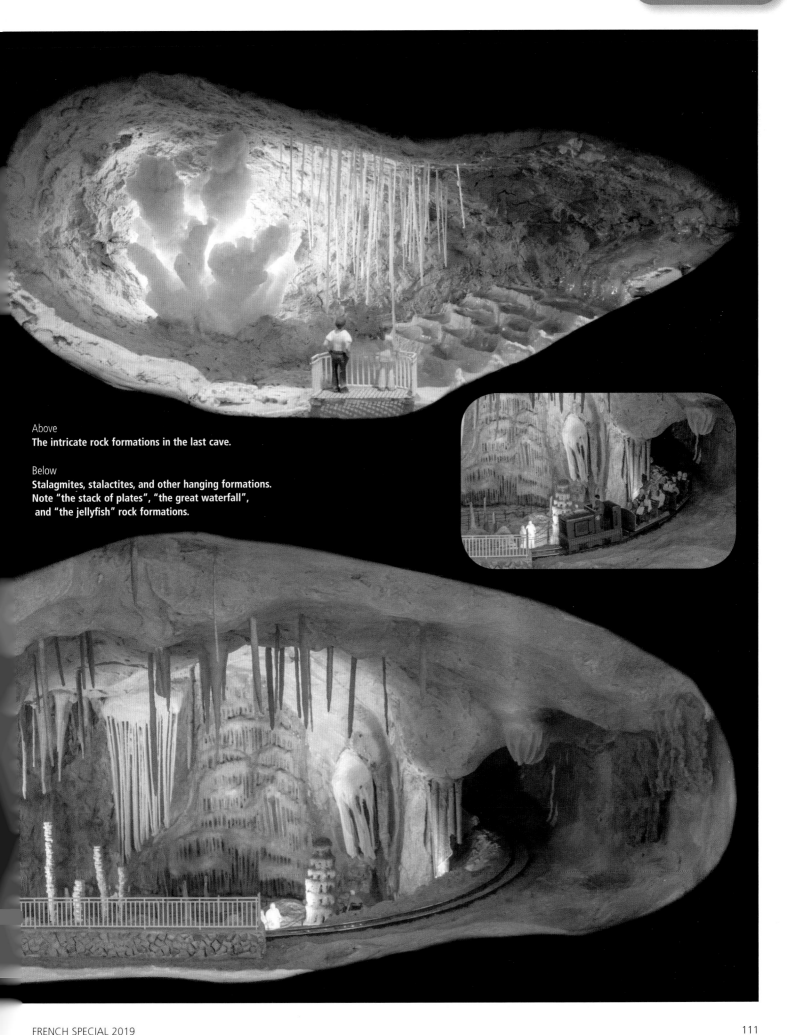

Above
The intricate rock formations in the last cave.

Below
Stalagmites, stalactites, and other hanging formations.
Note "the stack of plates", "the great waterfall",
 and "the jellyfish" rock formations.

# SNCF large C-C locos

**Gordon Wiseman** describes an interesting 'family' of French locomotives.
*Photographs by the author, or from his collection, unless noted otherwise.*

The CC6500 and CC21000 electrics and CC72000 diesels belong to the SNCF '*Nez Cassées*' (broken nose) design era which started with the quadruple supply system CC40101 in 1964 and concluded with the delivery of the last class BB22200 (22405) in 1986. The CC72000 were delivered 1967–74 and the CC6500 between 1969 and 1975 in three variants of body styling. Type 1 (6501 – 38) had full length horizontal bodyside grilles; type 2 (6539 – 59) had large plastic grilles; and type 3 (6560 – 74) had shallow offset stainless steel grilles.

As it has turned out, no six-axle locos have since been built for the SNCF, a similar situation to that in Britain and much of the rest of Europe where Co-Co locomotives have fallen out of favour as technology development allows ever more powerful four-axle locomotives.

Above
**SNCF quadruple supply
CC40105 at Brussels Midi
on 3rd April 1983
with a TEE service from Paris.**
Photo: Frank Hornby.

Left
**6546 in Maurienne green
hauls a Genève – Lyon
express formed of USI stock
through Vieux Bureau halt
near Meyrin (under the flight
path of Geneva airport).
This location is
unrecognisable today,
apart from the building
on the left which still exists
but is only recognisable
by its shape, having been
modernised and renamed
as Meyrin.**

Above
**6511 calls at Montauban with a Toulouse – Paris
*Capitole* 'Rapide' (ex-TEE) formed of Grand Confort coaches.**

According to the UIC wheel arrangement notation system, the 6500 and 72000 are C-C, not Co-Co, as they have a monomotor bogie. This often confuses viewers of the SNCF scene, not least because for years SNCF lettered locos with 'BB' and 'CC' to designate the number of axles regardless of the actual drive mechanism.

In an ironic twist for modellers, the monomotor bogie design makes the single motor bogie drive in old Lima models from the 1960s and 1970s an almost perfect replica, although most modellers would agree that the model design was far less successful than the real things!

## CC6500

Originally designed for top link and prestige passenger work, the CC6500 are often associated with the *Trans Europ Express* (TEE) trains on the former Paris – Orléans lines from Paris to south-west France, and similar prestige trains (such as the legendary *Mistral*) on the Paris Lyon Méditerranée route to Marseille. However, their high power was also designed to be useful for freight haulage on the whole of the French DC electrified network, and in particular type 2 was fitted from new with third rail shoes for dedicated use hauling both freight and passenger on the steeply graded Maurienne route towards Italy – electrified with third rail in 1925 at 1.5kV DC, the highest voltage ever used on a third rail system in Europe. In 1976 the third rail was replaced by overhead.

Between 1969 and 1976 a total of 74 were built, with the last of this class taken out of service in 2007. Four more were built as dual-system 1.5kV DC/25kV AC locomotives, classified CC21000. By 1997, these were reconfigured for use as DC-only, taking the total of CC6500s to 78.

As with most things SNCF, the combined effects of the spread of the TGV network reducing the need for locomotives, and the arrival of more modern universal high power locos affected the CC6500 which gradually lost their prestige work to other classes, culminating in their allocation to the freight sector from 1999. This saw some reliveried in the 'Fret' green livery which did not really sit well on them. However, their heavy freight capability kept them on the Maurienne route both as haulers and also banking engines.

Below
**6559 in the Fret livery, which really did not suit the splendid designer lines of the CC6500, standing at Lyon Perrache station in the latter days of CC6500 working on local passenger services around Lyon in the early 2000s.**

The persistent decline of SNCF freight operations has brought about several waves of rationalisation. That in 2004 resulted in the decision by the 'Fret' sector to withdraw the CC6500. However, the Rhône Alpes region saw a use for these locos and in 2006 eight were re-allocated to operate TER Rhône Alpes passenger services. As the class was very popular with enthusiasts both within and beyond France, this resulted in them enjoying a brief period of stardom as they were allocated to two or three small groups of easily identifiable rush hour TER services, making them easy to track and photograph. To add to the attraction, Rhône Alpes is a popular tourist area and most of the trains were on scenic routes through the Rhône Valley, the Alps, and the Jura mountains, including Lyon – Genève, Macon – Lyon – Avignon, and Lyon – Modane trains on the Maurienne line, so yet again keeping some locos originally fitted with third rail on that route.

## CC21000

Four CC21000 locos were built, 21001 and 002 in 1969 with the bodyside grilles equivalent to CC6500 type 1. 21003 and 004 followed in 1974 with grilles matching CC6500 type 3. Although there were only four, making them seem perhaps like prototype or test locos, they were deliberately built as two-system locos for powering trains from Paris to Switzerland via the Dijon – Vallorbe route, a task that did not really require more than four machines. They were similar enough to standard CC6500 to be eventually rebuilt as standard DC only machines in 1995-7 (thus extending the CC6500 number series to 6578).

Not so well known is that there was almost another variant of the CC6500, for AC, which would have been designated CC14500. This was never built as it was decided that services in the comparatively less hilly north and east of France could be covered by the B-B version of the *nez cassées* design then being developed, the BB15000, providing almost as much power but in a lighter locomotive.

Above
**21004 arriving at Paris with a train from Beograd in the early 1980s.**

Below
**6575, the former 21001 rebuilt into a plain CC6500 in 1996, at Macon.**

## CC72000 – the really big diesel

The CC72000 class was delivered from 1967. They took over top link trains on the major non-electrified SNCF routes – nearly all of which have since been electrified. Their presence and power has always endeared them to enthusiasts – apart from die-hard steam buffs, who decried them as replacements of the famous SNCF 241P Mountains.

For about twenty years they were unchallenged on express trains and on some specific freight routes where their power and route availability was useful.

Ordered in December 1965, the first of ninety-two was commissioned on 20th December 1967 at Rennes depot, and the last of the fleet was delivered on 21st June 1974.

Like the CC6500, the 72000 had monomotor bogies with gear selection.

The first twenty had a top speed of 140km/h, while the rest were geared for 160km/h. Both had the lower gear maximum speed of 85km/h designed for freight haulage but also used when hauling passenger trains over difficult routes such as the sinuous and steeply-graded Ligne des Sauvages on the Lyon – Nantes route and the Ligne des Alpes, which for a brief period in 1972 saw 72000s on a Grenoble – Marseille service via the 'mountain' route.

Introduced to replace express steam on trunk routes such as Le Mans – Nantes / Rennes – Brest/Quimper and the Paris – Clermont Ferrand Bourbonnais route, the CC72000s were allocated to just four depots through their lives – Rennes (1967-1992), Chalindrey (1969 – ), Vénissieux (1968-1992), and Nevers (1989-2012). However, despite their 'prestige' aura, their most high profile work only lasted around twenty years, between introduction in 1967 and the late 1980s.

The zenith of the 72000s was arguably on the *Trans Europ Express* (TEE) *Jules Verne* Paris to Nantes (395km) from September 1975, and on the TEE *Arbalète* Paris-Est to Basel from 1969 to 1979. They also held sway for twenty years on the Bourbonnais route which included haulage of the named trains of central France, most famously the *Thermal Express* serving the spa resorts of Vichy and Le Mont Dore. For some years they also reigned on the Nantes – La Rochelle – Bordeaux main line down the west coast of France, where they were replaced in the mid-1990s by pairs of BB67300 or 67400 diesels. For a period 72000 were used throughout between Grenoble and Nantes via Lyon, Bourges, Tours, Angers, and Saumur, a distance of some 760km.

Below
**72068 in 'Multiservice' grey on Line 4 to Belfort in the first rural countryside after leaving the Paris conurbation**

Above
**72035 at Chaumont with a Paris – Culmont Chalindrey train in November 2002**

Below
**72063 passes near Vesaignes sur Marne on the Marne valley line known as 'Line 4' from Paris to Mulhouse and Basel. 1997.**

Left
72049 double headed
with 72074 on a Roanne
commuter working at Tarare
in October 2003

Below
72130 storms towards
Port sur Saone with a
Mulhouse – Paris express
in June 2012.

Right
72148 on a test run
from Chalindrey works
at Chaumont in 'phantom'
livery, just after being
rebuilt from 72048.

Below
In June 2012, 72145 with a
southbound express passes
La Ferté sur Amance with
its characteristic unusual
heavy duty telegraph poles.

They gradually lost out to ever-expanding electrification, particularly in the 1987–1990 period when the Brittany routes went over to TGV as part of the TGV Atlantique, and Paris – Clermont was electrified using BB22200 electrics as straight replacements for 72000s. For a while they also hauled trains to the Channel coast from Amiens.

In their latter years, having lost work to electrification and TGVs, they became better known by enthusiasts for work which they were already doing but to which more attention was then paid. This included heavy freights south from Luxembourg, and cross-country freight from Dijon to Nevers and Clermont-Ferrand, while passenger services included Paris – Laon (until 2002) and cross–country trains, some covering long distances such as Bordeaux – Lyon over the scenic central French route via Ussel and Brive-la-Gaillarde, and Reims – Dijon via Chalons-en-Champagne, a route which parallels the 'route des anglais' road route from Calais to Geneva in Switzerland. They were the regular traction on the Genève – Valence via Grenoble route so were well known to Swiss enthusiasts as they also appeared several times a day at Basel on passenger trains from Paris Est via Mulhouse, and on freight.

In fact they also visited another station in Switzerland – Delle, in the days when Paris – Bern through coaches ran into Switzerland from Belfort. The CC72000 having hauled a Paris – Basel train to Belfort would remove the two Swiss coaches and shunt them into a bay. A BB15000 electric would take over the remaining Paris – Basel coaches and take them off to Basel via Mulhouse – electrified since 1970.

The 72000 would then (easily…) haul the two Swiss coaches across the border into Delle where they were coupled up to a Swiss internal service.

Having lost passenger work, on the introduction of business sectorisation by SNCF in 1999 many 72000s were allocated to the Fret sector and repainted in the green livery. Six of these were later sold to Morocco where they run alongside equivalents delivered new to ONCF. The ex-SNCF locos are still running in Fret green but with logos removed.

In the meantime time three of the class regained prestige status when 72061, 72062, and 72064 were equipped with special couplings (as were the TGV sets) in 2000 to pull Paris – Les Sables-d'Olonne TGV Atlantique trains beyond Nantes to the Vendée coast. These 'TGV Vendée' survived untll 11th December 2004. The hauled TGVs were replaced by cross platform connections at Nantes. The 72000 still hauled the replacement services, albeit now formed of moribund 1960s coaches of the UIC and USI types in their distinctive green and grey livery. This developed for a time in to a small network of 72000-hauled commuter services between Nantes and the coast.

The same combination of loco and stock was used for a good few years on long distance peak period services west of Lyon where their power was useful for hauling well-loaded commuter trains in hilly territory, notably on the runs to and from Roanne via two different routes. For a time this made Lyon – Roanne something of a hotbed of 72000 use, with the commuter trains joining 72000-hauled inter city trains on the Lyon – Tours – Nantes route.

The last daily regular use of CC72000s was on remnants of this once important cross-France route, on Tours – Lyon services, and some associated shorter commuter-orientated hops such as Tours – Nevers. Because of their reduced daily mileage, the three 'TGV Vendée' machines were among the last four 72000s in commercial service, which ended on 13th December 2009.

In contrast to the original 72000s, most of the thirty locos refurbished and re-engined as CC72100 in 2002-4 are still in service. All are based at Chalindrey depot as almost all their work is on the Paris – Mulhouse 'Line 4'. On refurbishment all were painted in the 'En Voyage' livery for inter-city passenger use. Their days are probably now numbered due to electrification of the Paris – Troyes section of this line.

The three remaining 'genuine' 72000s (049, 074, and 084) were also all allocated to Chalindrey, and to the 'Materiel' (traction/rolling stock) sector. They are kept in reserve and used occasionally for moving stock from one place to another around France. 049 and 074, which also received 'En Voyage' livery in their latter days as passenger locos, still occasionally appear on 72100 turns. 72084 is more often to be seen on the ad-hoc materiel duties, and appears very regularly at heritage events, often accompanying and/or acting as a reserve for steam locomotives. 72013, which I saw for myself at Chalindrey depot in June 2012, has been withdrawn.

## Oddities

72061, 062, and 064 would be a good subject for the model manufacturers as they retained their early 1980s livery until the end, so one of them could be used on a layout covering late 2000s as well as late 1980s allowing their uise with a wide variety of coach liveries and wagon types. 72064 has been preserved by ARCET since August 2010. It was the last original, AGO-engined loco to be used in regular service.

72006 along with 67373 are the only SNCF locos ever to carry the blue variant of the SNCF 'Multiservice' livery (known as 'Isabelle' as the colour is officially *bleu Isabelle*). Roco reproducing this loco in model form will have pleased some and irritated others: a better option would be to produce the more widely used red stripe version of this livery, as Jouef have done.

72030 is unique in having carryied four liveries: the original blue, French *tricouleur* livery in 1989 in commemoration of the bicentennial of the French Revolution, 'Multiservice' red, grey, and silver, and now the 'En Voyage' livery as 72130, one of those converted to 72100 class. It is also the French diesel loco with the highest mileage since its commissioning (about 7 million).

72084 has been preserved in 'heritage' livery with its original metal raised numerals. It has hauled various exhibition and promotional trains, such as in 2006 when it took the 'Train de Rugby' all around France promoting the 2007 Rugby World Cup.

## Super-detail in 1:35

**Christian Labuch**
created two cameo scenes.

# Mini scenes

At the *Model Trein Expo – OntraXS!* in the Dutch national railway museum in Utrecht in March 2019, noted German modeller Christian Labuch displayed alongside his impressive *Hinterlassenschaften Hamburg '46* 1:35 layout a couple of small dioramas with French themes.

One used forced perspective to recreate a well-known Dubonnet advertisement, featuring a Citroën 2CV and a VéloSolex moped, the other shows a Citroën type H van converted to a sales stand, along with its environs and clientèle.

The amazing level of detail speaks for itself.

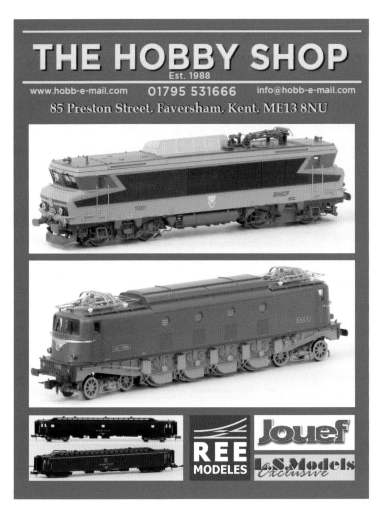

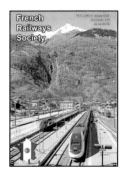

# GAUGEMASTER
## NEW Website

Our existing website has been withdrawn from service, which was a sad moment for us here as it has served us (and you) well over the years.

The online world has changed massively over the last few years and we've listened to all of your feedback about the old site as we developed our new version, and therefore invite you to take a look at our new site.

## www.gaugemaster.com

We feel that the biggest improvements are in the following areas:

- It's been **built with mobile in mind**.
  Mobile devices have now overtaken desktop devices for internet browsing. We needed to follow this trend.
- It **demonstrates our breadth of products**.
  All of our genres (railways, slot cars, kits etc.) are now under one online roof. We stock products from around the world.
- **Easier navigation**.
  Simpler ways to find the products you want, including numerous new search filters.
- **Better and more images**.
  Multi angle, high resolution pictures of the products that interest you.
- **A more powerful search box**.
  This will be your closest companion on our new site.
- An **Events listing**.
  Things that might interest you locally such as exhibitions or shows.
- A '**Club Hub**'.
  This is where we highlight clubs and societies where you can meet like-minded people.

This project was a massive undertaking, and we'd like to think we've got a lot of it right.
However, we REALLY welcome your feedback by email **customerservices@gaugemaster.com**, or by telephone on **01903 884488**, so please do get in touch with your comments.

**We look forward to welcoming you to our new (online) home!**

*The powerful search tools at the top of the page will allow you to find what you want quickly and easily.*

*Extended descriptions and multiple images mean that you can find out everything about a product before commiting to buy.*

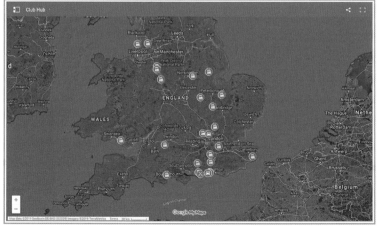

*The Club Hub pinpoints modelling clubs around the country, and the events listing shows upcoming exhibitions.*

---

GAUGEMASTER products are available from your local model shop or, in case of difficulty, direct from ourselves
**GAUGEMASTER** Controls Ltd, Ford Road, Arundel, West Sussex, BN18 0BN, United Kingdom
tel - 01903 884488 fax - 01903 884377 email - sales@gaugemaster.com

## www.gaugemaster.com